MW01033778

elements
of
FORTRAN
style:

techniques
for
effective
programming

CHARLES B. KREITZBERG
Educational Testing Service, Princeton

BEN SHNEIDERMAN
*State University of New York,
Agricultural and Technical College, Farmingdale*

HARCOURT BRACE JOVANOVICH, INC.
New York   Chicago   San Francisco   Atlanta

To our parents

ISBN: 0-15-522156-6

Library of Congress Catalog Card Number: 77-188964

Printed in the United States of America

PREFACE

The attributes of a well-written computer program are evident. It is efficient, fast, well documented, elegant, and, of course, correct. How to write such a program is not so obvious. By presenting essential techniques of FORTRAN style, this book teaches the art of writing a good program. Each technique is carefully explained and the rationale for it is given so that the student can learn when to apply a rule and when to develop his own. It is our hope that *The Elements of FORTRAN Style* will enable the novice programmer to become a good one and the good programmer to become a better one.

We are grateful for the detailed reviews of Paul Siegel, Instructional Resources Center, SUNY, Stony Brook, and Charles Thompson, SUNY, Farmingdale. We also thank the following for their helpful comments and suggestions: David Beaucage, Rutgers; Garth Bracewell, Empire State College; Gerald Chandler, RCA Laboratories; Michael Feldman, Educational Testing Services; Richard Kieburtz, SUNY, Stony Brook; Irving Rabinowitz, Rutgers; Norman Rubin, CUNY; Susan Silvera, SUNY, Farmingdale; and Stuart Wecker, SUNY, Stony Brook.

Charles B. Kreitzberg
Ben Shneiderman

CONTENTS

CHAPTER 1

INTRODUCTION

In 1919, a Cornell University professor, William Strunk, published a remarkable book which he called *The Elements of Style*.[1] In only 44 pages Professor Strunk laid down a comprehensive set of rules for literary style. In this book, we present a guide to good style for programmers, not prose writers. Our goal is to help you write better programs.

The similarities between program structure and prose structure are striking. Both programs written in computer language and prose built from natural language have rules of spelling and sentence formation. Variables in computer languages correspond to nouns in natural languages, operators have their counterpart in verbs, arithmetic expressions resemble phrases, statements resemble sentences, and subroutines are similar to paragraphs. Consider the following maxims which are set down in *The Elements of Style*:

- work from a suitable design
- be clear
- revise and rewrite

[1] Now available in revised edition, W. S. Strunk, Jr. and E. B. White, *The Elements of Style*, Macmillan, 1959.

- do not take shortcuts at the expense of clarity
- omit needless words
- prefer the standard to the offbeat
- do not use dialect
- do not overwrite

These rules provide a basis for defining programming style.

Style is subjective. As programmers, we rarely share a common background because of the variations among compiler dialects, operating systems, hardware configurations, and programming environments. These variations make it impossible to specify a complete, consistent, and universal set of programming rules. In consequence, programming style must be approached functionally. Each programmer must decide which rules, conscientiously applied, will produce the type of program he desires. As in prose, the best effect is sometimes achieved by deliberate transgression of a rule. For these reasons, the rationale underlying the rules presented in this book is carefully explained; hopefully you will be able to apply the rules intelligently and appropriately.

A *correct* program is one that produces the desired results. Obviously, a "good" program must be correct. There are usually many correct programs that will solve a particular problem; of these some may be faster than others, some may be more accurate than others, some will require less storage than others, some will be beautifully structured and easy to modify. The ideal program would embody all these qualities. However, there are very few ideal programs in the real world, because the factors which make a program "good" are not mutually independent. Increasing computational efficiency will often produce an increase in the storage requirement. Elegant algorithms are often difficult to understand. Thus, style must always be tempered by the programming environment. The programmer who has a mini-computer will almost certainly have different design goals from the programmer with a gigantic "number cruncher" at his disposal. Deadlines, too, often force a programmer to write hastily for the most elegant program is useless until it is running.

What then, should be the goal? To write the best possible program in the available time using the available resources. As far as possible the program should be accurate, well-documented, frugal in its use of storage, computationally efficient, modular, and compiler independent. Consider some of Professor Strunk's rules and how they apply to program construction.

Work from a suitable design.

Without careful planning, a program will become a disaster when it comes to debugging and modifying. A cant word used by programmers to describe programs held together by faith and patches is *kludge*. Don't create kludges! The temptation to begin coding a program fragment is tremendous but must be overcome. Programs should be modular, with well-conceived notions of the function of each subprogram and program fragment. The organization should be logical and meaningful so that debugging is easy.

Be clear.

You are not the only person who will read your program, and six months after you complete the program you will have forgotten what you did, anyway. It takes very little time to insert comments into a program listing and to choose meaningful variable and subprogram names. A program is not complete until good documentation is available.

Revise and rewrite.

After writing a program, go through it. Do you expect it to run correctly? Is it understandable? Could you make it more efficient? If there is substantial room for improvement (there usually is) and if the program is not modular (it usually isn't), then revisions should be considered.

Do not take shortcuts at the expense of clarity.

Shortcuts usually lead to trouble; they rarely pay off. If you absolutely must take shortcuts, carefully document your intent and check with someone else to see if your explanation is comprehensible. Don't be clever for the sake of being clever — the computer can't appreciate it anyway.

Omit needless words.

To paraphrase Professor Strunk "vigorous programming is concise. A statement should contain no unnecessary computations, a routine no unnecessary statements, for the same reason that a drawing should have no unnecessary lines and a machine no unnecessary parts." Make every statement count.

Prefer the standard to the offbeat.

How we programmers love to be clever and cute. How proud we are when we discover some strange and unusual way to save a few bits or microseconds. As an example of what not to do consider the (true) case of a programmer who, in writing part of an operating system, saved one byte of storage by using the operation code of an instruction as a constant. He reasoned that the op-code had to be there anyway and that he was lucky that it was exactly the number he needed. Later when the op-code was changed, it took weeks to discover why the program was producing incorrect results.

Do not use dialect.

The number of different versions of FORTRAN, each with its own idiosyncrasies and advantages, makes this difficult. It is tempting to use statements unique to your system, since they may offer advantages in simplicity and efficiency. However, the cost of creating a compiler-dependent program may be great since transferring the program to another system will be difficult, tedious, and unsure. The American National Standards Institute (ANSI) has defined the FORTRAN language, and programs which adhere to the ANSI standard will compile on any FORTRAN system.

Do not overwrite.

There is a limit to how much effort should be spent on a program. Don't try to squeeze out every excess instruction or every wasted location. There is a point of diminishing returns after which additional effort is wasted.

These rules are basic to good programming. Programs may have frills, embroidery, and gold trimming but should not have excessive, wasteful, or unnecessary statements. Each programmer must decide whether his program is suitable for the environment in which he works. Only by understanding the hardware, the software, and the job requirements is it possible to evaluate the quality of a program.

As you consider these rules you will realize that program style and prose style have much in common. However, we should not strain the analogy. Many stylistic factors are unique to programming languages. Some of these are techniques — methods of accomplishing a specific task; others are more general. Chapters 2 and 3 present techniques which may be applicable to specific situations. The remainder of the book is concerned with more general stylistic considerations. There is rarely an absolute standard of "goodness" which can be applied to programs. It is usually a question of how appropriate a program is within the context of its environment.

PROBLEM-ORIENTED LANGUAGES

We begin our study of programming style by considering the transformation of a set of FORTRAN statements into an executable program. Computers cannot directly execute FORTRAN programs since the high-level FORTRAN instructions differ considerably, in format and complexity, from the low-level machine instructions. Prior to execution, a FORTRAN program (*source program*) must be translated into machine instructions. The first stage, called *compilation*, is the translation from the programmer's source code to the equivalent machine language program. In the second stage, called *linkage editing*,[2] the compiled FORTRAN program (*object program*) is combined with independently compiled subroutines to produce a complete executable program. When this executable program is loaded, it is ready to be run.

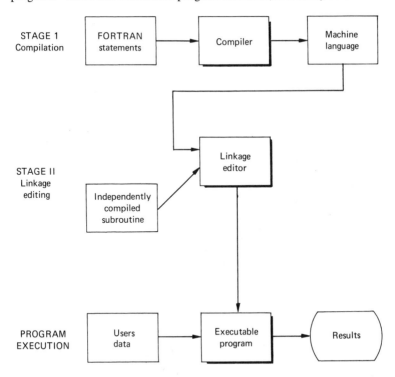

---

[2]On some computers the process of linkage editing is known as "loading." However, "loading" is also used for several other processes and the term is best avoided in this context.

In the process of compilation, the FORTRAN expression

$$Y = A*B + C/D$$

might be translated into machine instructions as follows:

CLA	A	Clear the accumulator[3] and add in the value of A
MPY	B	Multiply the value of A by the value of B
STO	T	Store the intermediate result in location T
CLA	C	Clear the accumulator and add in the value of C
DIV	D	Divide the value of C by the value of D
ADD	T	Add the value of T to the quotient
STO	Y	Store the result in location Y

More complex tasks such as exponentiation or taking the square root require dozens of operations to be performed. Input or output of data may require thousands of operations on the part of the machine. The translation from *source code* (high-level language instructions) to *object code* (low-level machine instructions) is a difficult and tedious task best left to the compiler. However, an understanding of the nature of the translation process is helpful to the programmer who seeks to write the elusive "good" program.

Compilers enable the programmer to consider his problem in terms with which he is familiar and permit him to ignore the specific details of the particular machine with which he is working. Unfortunately, compilers also separate the programmer from the executable program.

---

[3] An accumulator, as the name implies, is a special location in a computer used to accumulate arithmetic results.

As a result, it is often difficult to anticipate the outcome of a decision without a detailed knowledge of the compiler and the operating system. Nonetheless, coding in a high level is preferred to coding in low-level machine instructions for most applications.

The number of high-level languages is staggering. The first (1956) and by far the most popular and widespread is FORTRAN. The name was taken from the phrase FORmula TRANslation, since the language was designed to aid programmers in coding mathematical problems. FORTRAN has gone through several modifications, and assorted dialects have arisen. To bring order out of the resultant chaos, ANSI proposed, in 1966, two standard sets of instructions called Basic FORTRAN IV and FORTRAN IV. Although nonstandard versions of FORTRAN such as WATFOR, WATFIV, and CONFOR exist, the computer industry has made an effort to adhere to the ANSI standard in its implementations of FORTRAN.

Algorithmic languages similar to FORTRAN have been developed in the past 15 years including MAD (Michigan Algorithmic Decoder), ALGOL (ALGOrithmic Language), and two languages especially designed for time sharing, BASIC (Beginner's All Purpose Symbolic Instruction Code) and FOCAL (Formulating On-Line Calculations in Algebraic Language). Remote terminals also motivated the development of APL (A Programming Language), which has a concise mathematically oriented notation which minimizes the number of keystrokes. The advanced techniques of list processing and recursive function invocation were embedded in the syntax of the LISP (LISt Processing) programming language. Recursive functions were also incorporated in SNOBOL (String Oriented Symbolic Language), which was developed to simplify the manipulation of character strings.

In 1960, the business programming community produced COBOL (COmmon Business Oriented Language) to ease the processing of extensive files of data in accounting applications. Later the RPG (Report Program Generator) language was created for simple business-oriented uses.

An attempt was made to reduce the divergence between scientific and business languages by the creation of PL/I (Programming Language No. 1) in the mid-1960's. This complex sophisticated language allegedly contains the best of FORTRAN and COBOL. It was hoped that PL/I would eventually replace the other languages. However, the investment in FORTRAN and COBOL has proved to be so great that there is reluctance to switch to PL/I.

Our emphasis is on FORTRAN IV, but many of the concepts apply to other languages.

DEVELOPMENT OF A PROGRAM

Computers are used as tools to solve problems, and the best programmers are those who understand both the areas of application and
the intricacies of computer usage.

Clarifying what the problem is can be most difficult: It requires
a keen understanding of the terminology and techniques of a particular
problem area. Generally there is more than one way to solve a problem,
and it may be difficult to identify the best way. When a particular route
has been chosen, the next step is to formalize the technique by drawing
a flowchart or writing out the steps of an algorithm in algebraic and
English phrases. At this point the problem-related language-independent
details should be resolved so that a researcher in the application area
would be able to follow the steps of the solution.

The second phase of the problem-solving process is to implement
the algorithm in terms of a programming language such as FORTRAN.
The instructions are then keypunched or entered into the computer
through a terminal. Next the tedious tasks of debugging, testing, and
final documenting must be accomplished before the program can be
accepted as complete.

The two phases of formalization of the problem in terms of a flowchart or algorithm and of implementation of the algorithm in a programming language are not independent. Psychologists have long main-
tained that language molds thinking, arguing that it seems to be impossible to think without using words or symbols. Similarly it is not
possible to develop an algorithm without being influenced by the nature
of the programming language being used. There are strong similarities
among the languages, but the features of a particular language may
have a profound influence on the algorithm that is created. The avail-
ability of sophisticated data structures, special operators or functions,
or list-processing facilities may reduce the difficulty of implementing
a complicated algorithm.

If a critical design goal is to minimize execution time, then a complex but fast algorithm is in order. If storage space is at a premium,
effort should be applied to eliminate useless information and to compact the remaining data. If development time is limited or if other
programmers may modify your code, the simplest and most obvious
algorithm should be selected.

Novice programmers eagerly implement the first technique that
comes to mind and worry about resolving difficulties after a few runs.

The temptation to begin keypunching and get results is great, but it must be overcome. Professional programmers carefully consider alternative methods and design the entire program before they code a single line. A few minutes of extra thought at the early stages of problem solving can save a great deal of effort at the later stages. *A think in time saves nine.*

Example

Tracing the conversion of a correct but poor program into a "good" program is instructive. The following commonly written program demonstrates many of the principles that we wish to encourage.

The program reads a set of 413 data items ranging from 001 to 100 (possibly student grades) and prints out a frequency distribution for the number of items in each of the intervals

$$001-010$$
$$011-020$$
$$\vdots$$
$$091-100$$

Program 1 works but lacks generality, is poorly documented, is not efficient in terms of execution time or storage utilization, and produces numerical printout intelligible only to the programmer.

```
      DIMENSION MK(1000),NS(10)
      DO 7 I = 1,10
 7    NS(I)=0
      DO 69 I = 1,413
 69   READ(1,91)  MK(I)
 91   FORMAT( I4)
      DO 34 J = 1,413
      IF( MK(J) .GE.1.AND.MK(J).LE. 10) NS(1) = NS(1)+1
      IF( MK(J).GE.11.AND.MK(J).LE. 20) NS(2) = NS(2)+1
      IF( MK(J).GE.21.AND.MK(J).LE. 30) NS(3) = NS(3)+1
      IF( MK(J).GE.31.AND.MK(J).LE. 40) NS(4) = NS(4)+1
      IF( MK(J).GE.41.AND.MK(J).LE. 50) NS(5) = NS(5)+1
      IF( MK(J).GE.51.AND.MK(J).LE. 60) NS(6) = NS(6)+1
      IF( MK(J).GE.61.AND.MK(J).LE. 70) NS(7) = NS(7)+1
      IF( MK(J).GE.71.AND.MK(J).LE. 80) NS(8) = NS(8)+1
      IF( MK(J).GE.81.AND.MK(J).LE. 90) NS(9) = NS(9)+1
      IF( MK(J).GE.91.AND.MK(J).LE.100) NS(10) = NS(10) + 1
 34   CONTINUE
      DO 103 I=1, 10
103   WRITE(3,47) NS(I)
 47   FORMAT(1H , I6)
      CALL EXIT
      END
```

This program is typical of the kind of work found among novices. With a little more effort and some thought, the programmer might have turned out a better job. The heart of the program is the DO 34 loop with ten entries. Such inefficient programming could easily be improved by using an inner DO loop and only testing on the upper bound of the interval. More meaningful variable names could be used, statement numbers could be chosen more thoughtfully, and comments could be inserted. Finally, the printed results could be displayed in tabular form. Now look at Program 2.

```
C         THIS PROGRAM READS 413 STUDENT GRADES AND DETERMINES THE
C         FREQUENCY DISTRIBUTION
C
&         PROGRAMMER - BEN G. RYAN
C
C         DATE - JUNE 6, 1944
C
      DIMENSION MARKS(1000),NCLASS(10)
C
C         INITIALIZE COUNTERS TO ZERO
C
      DO 10 I = 1,10
   10 NCLASS(I) = 0
C
C         INPUT DATA
C
      DO 20 I = 1,413
   20 READ(1,100) MARKS(I)
  100 FORMAT(I4)
C
C         DETERMINE PROPER INTERVAL FOR EACH ITEM
C
      DO 40 I = 1,413
      DO 30 LIM = 10,100,10
      IF(MARKS(I) .LE. LIM) GO TO 35
   30 CONTINUE
   35 J = LIM/10
      NCLASS(J) = NCLASS(J) + 1
   40 CONTINUE
C
C         PRINT HEADING
C
      WRITE(3,101)
  101 FORMAT('1    INTERVAL      NUMBER',
     1      '+   _____      _____'/)
C
C         PRINT FREQUENCY DISTRIBUTION TABLE
C
      DO 50 I = 1,10
      NHI = 10*I
      NLO = NHI - 9
      WRITE(3,102) NLO,NHI,NCLASS(I)
  102 FORMAT('  ', I3, ' - ', I3, 6X, I3)
   50 CONTINUE
      CALL EXIT
      END
```

Version two is better, but there is still room for improvement. The inner DO 30 loop which tests for membership in each interval could be replaced by a clever transformation. Simply divide the mark by 10 to determine which interval it belongs to, thus eliminating code and creating a faster program.

The program could be made more general by making the number of data items a variable which is read in. The input could be reorganized to have more items per card, and the input DO 20 loop could be changed to an implied DO loop. The "integrity" of the program could be improved by adding a test to determine if the marks are within the proper range. Finally, look at Program 3, on the facing page.

This too is not the perfect program. It could be converted into a subroutine and made more general by making the range, number of intervals, and I/O units variable. If this routine were to be used repeatedly by a number of people, these details would be worth considering; otherwise they are excess icing which does not add to the flavor.

SOCIAL RESPONSIBILITY

The "goodness" of a program cannot be measured only in narrow technical terms. Although good programming practice includes minimizing the storage space required, reducing the execution time, and creating a modular well-documented program, a broader view is necessary. Programmers must go beyond purely technical details and consider the impact of their work. The most compelling design goal is to produce a program that performs its required task with maximum benefit and minimum disadvantage. For example, an efficient university registration system should not only allow the student a choice in section assignments but should also allow for late registration or course changes. Programmers of credit information systems must verify the validity of the input data to ensure that no one inadvertently or incorrectly receives a poor credit rating. The developers of automated billing systems must work diligently to guarantee that no customer is improperly charged and that mistakes can be easily remedied. Computerized systems must be used to expand our choices and options, not to create a rigid controlled society.

Perhaps the most important message is that a "good" program is written by a "good" programmer — one who not only considers the mechanics of a program but also its effects.

```
C
C          THIS PROGRAM READS A SINGLE CONTROL CARD TO DETERMINE HOW MANY
C          DATA ITEMS FOLLOW.  THE FREQUENCY DISTRIBUTION FOR THE DATA
C          ITEMS IS DETERMINED AND PRINTED.
C
C          PROGRAMMER - A. HAMILTON
C
C          DATE - JULY 4, 1776
C
C
       DIMENSION MARKS(1000),NCLASS(10)
C
C          INITIALIZE COUNTERS TO ZERO
C
       DO 10 I = 1,10
   10 NCLASS(I) = 0
C
C          INPUT NUMBER OF DATA ITEMS
C
       READ(1,100) N
  100 FORMAT(I4)
C
C          INPUT N DATA ITEMS
C
       READ(1,101) (MARKS(I), I = 1,N)
  101 FORMAT(20I4)
C
C          LOOP FOR EACH DATA ITEM
C
       DO 40 I = 1,N
C
C          TEST IF DATA IS IN RANGE
C
       IF (MARKS(I) .LT. 1 .OR. MARKS(I) .GT. 100) GO TO 30
C
C          TRANSFORMATION TO DIRECTLY DETERMINE CLASS INTERVAL MEMBERSHIP
C
       J = MARKS(I) - 1/10 + 1
       NCLASS(J) = NCLASS(J) + 1
       GO TO 40
   30 WRITE(3,102) MARKS(I)
  102 FORMAT(' ***MKS001 - DATA OUT OF RANGE ', I12)
   40 CONTINUE
C
C          PRINT HEADING
C
       WRITE(3,103)
  103 FORMAT('1    INTERVAL      NUMBER',
      1       '+    _____      _____'/)
C
C          PRINT FREQUENCY DISTRIBUTION TABLE
C
       DO 50 I = 1,10
       NHI = 10*I
       NLO = NHI - 9
       WRITE(3,104) NLO,NHI,NCLASS(I)
  104 FORMAT('   ', I3, ' - ', I3, 6X, I3)
   50 CONTINUE
       CALL EXIT
       END
```

Checklist

Program structure
- Is the organization of your program modular?
- Does each routine and subroutine perform a well-defined, complete function?
- Is the program's flow straightforward?
- Does it go from top to bottom instead of jumping around?

Dialect
- Have you avoided special statements peculiar to your particular version of FORTRAN?
- Have you employed machine language subroutines? Are they needed?

Program development
- Have you chosen the best algorithm for the environment in which your program will be run?
- Have you written flowcharts on both the macro and the detailed level?
- Is your program general?
- Can it be used easily with new data?

CHAPTER 2

REDUCING PROGRAM COMPUTE TIME

INTRODUCTION

The *run time* of a computer program is the sum of three parts: *compute time* — the time needed to execute the instructions in the program; *voluntary wait time* — the time that a program must wait for the completion of an event which it initiated (such as an input-output operation); and *involuntary wait time* — the time that a program must wait due to other programs in a multiprogramming environment. The run time of a program may be expressed as the following equation:

$$\text{Run time} = \text{compute time} + \text{voluntary wait time} + \text{involuntary wait time}$$

Decreasing the run time of a program is desirable, because computer time is expensive. A programmer may reduce the compute time and the voluntary wait time to good effect. Involuntary wait time, since it is a function of the operating environment, is not usually amenable to programmer modification.

Unfortunately, decreasing the compute time of a program will sometimes increase the storage requirements, the voluntary wait time, and, almost certainly, the programming effort. In determining the effort which should be devoted to reducing the compute time of a program, the factors to be considered are

- The number of times that the program will be run
- The savings in compute time which can be realized
- The development time available
- The complexity of the program
- The cost of computer time
- The cost of programmer time
- The trade-off with respect to storage and voluntary wait time

It may not be reasonable to expend a great deal of effort to achieve a relatively small reduction in compute time, especially in a short program to be run only once. On the other hand, a frequently executed routine such as a library subprogram or a complex, long-running program may benefit from extensive analysis.

When attempting to reduce computer time, you should consider the selection of an efficient algorithm, proper program structure, and careful construction of the source statements. This chapter summarizes these techniques and provides rules for eliminating superfluous and redundant code. Several programming techniques which may increase computational efficiency are also described. Reduction of the program's storage requirements is discussed in Chapter 3.

ELIMINATING REDUNDANT EXPRESSIONS

One of the most frequent causes of computational inefficiency is the calculation of unnecessary expressions. Some compilers are able to detect and correct these faults at the expense of increased compile time. Since one of the advantages of "high-level" languages is computer independence, do not rely upon the existence of a sophisticated compiler to optimize your programs; especially since the optimizing compiler may not always be available. Of course, a "smart" compiler should be employed when available, since even the most sophisticated program may benefit from compile-time optimization.

It is often difficult to determine the extent and nature of the optimization provided by a given compiler. Compilers such as WATFOR and IBM OS/360 FORTRAN G provide very little optimization; however, the IBM OS/360 FORTRAN H performs extensive optimization. As a rule, it is best to eliminate redundant computations when doing so provides a reasonable return for the effort expended.

Arithmetic Expressions

Consider the familiar formula for solution of a quadratic equation:

$$r_1, r_2 = \frac{-b \pm \sqrt{b^2 - 4ac}}{2a}$$

The two roots of the equation (r_1 and r_2) may be successfully computed by transliterating the above formula into the following FORTRAN statements:

```
R1 = (-B + SQRT(B ** 2. - 4.0 * A * C)) / (2.0 * A)
R2 = (-B - SQRT(B ** 2. - 4.0 * A * C)) / (2.0 * A)
```

On a commonly used compiler,[1] the above statements required

    4 subprogram calls
    8 multiplications and divisions
    4 additions and subtractions
   21 load, store, and branch instructions

for evaluation. The above transliteration thus involves a considerable amount of redundancy due to the unnecessary recomputation of common subexpressions. The value

$$b^2 - 4ac$$

(the discriminant) need be computed only once:

```
DISCR = B ** 2. - 4. * A * C
R1 = (-B + SQRT(DISCR)) / ( 2.0 * A)
R2 = (-B - SQRT(DISCR)) / ( 2.0 * A)
```

[1] IBM OS/360 FORTRAN G.

If the value of the discriminant is not required as such elsewhere in the program, the two function calls to SQRT may, similarly, be reduced to one, and the redundant computation of the subexpression 2.0 * A may be eliminated:

```
DENOM = 2.0 * A
SDISCR = SQRT(B ** 2. - 4. * A * C)
R1 = (-B + SDISCR) / DENOM
R2 = (-B - SDISCR) / DENOM
```

The redundant subexpression —B is probably not worth eliminating, since most computers have a fast *negate* command in their instruction set. More subtly, the multiplication in DENOM may be replaced by an (faster) addition, and the exponentiation in SDISCR may be replaced by a multiplication (eliminating a possible subroutine call):

```
DENOM = A + A
SDISCR = SQRT(B * B - 4.0 * A * C)
R1 = (-B + SDISCR) / DENOM
R2 = (-B - SDISCR) / DENOM
```

This final computation involves

> 1 subprogram call
> 5 multiplications and divisions
> 4 additions and subtractions
> 16 load, store, and branch instructions

and is considerably more efficient than the original expression. Compile time is also reduced by 25 percent. This example is one in which the optimization would probably not be worth the effort, because the original transliteration does not require much compute time. If, however, the calculation of quadratic roots must be performed many times, the total time saved will make the effort well worth it.

A more subtle example of concealed redundancy may be found in the following program segment which computes the volumes of a cylinder, a cone, and a sphere:

$$V_{\text{cylinder}} = \pi r^2 h \qquad V_{\text{cone}} = \frac{\pi r^2 h}{3} \qquad V_{\text{sphere}} = \frac{4}{3}\pi r^3$$

```
VCYL = PI * RADIUS ** 2 * HEIGHT
VCONE = PI * HEIGHT * RADIUS ** 2 / 3.0
VSPHER = 4.0 / 3.0 * PI * RADIUS ** 3
```

The program segment above may be written more efficiently as

```
ACIRC = PI * RADIUS * RADIUS
VCYL = ACIRC * HEIGHT
VCONE = VCYL * 0.333333
VSPHER = 1.33333 * ACIRC * RADIUS
```

Note that in both examples, the increased efficiency has been accompanied by a reduction in the clarity of the algorithm employed. For this reason, it is necessary to carefully document such changes; Chapter 5 discusses documentation considerations in detail.

The elimination of redundant subexpressions can be summarized by the following rule:

If an expression does not change value between multiple occurrences of that expression then it should be evaluated only once and its value assigned to a new variable which replaces all subsequent occurrences of the original expression.

You must be certain that none of the variables in the common subexpression changes value between occurrences of the subexpression. A double check should be made of variables which are arguments of subroutines, occur in COMMON, or are EQUIVALENCE'd, to other variables.

Notice that certain arithmetic operators have been replaced by others for increased execution speed. The details of instruction times must be gleaned from manufacturer's manuals, but the following general rules apply:

- INTEGER arithmetic is faster than REAL arithmetic, and REAL arithmetic is faster than DOUBLE PRECISION arithmetic.
- Addition and subtraction are faster than multiplication.
- Multiplication is faster than division.
- Exponentiation is very slow and is usually performed by a library subroutine.

Polynomial Factoring (Horner's Method)

If a polynomial is to be evaluated many times, it may be factored to reduce the amount of computation.

For example, the polynomial $Y = 5X^3 + 7X^2 + 6X + 2$ could be evaluated as

```
Y = 5.0*X*X*X + 7.0*X*X + 6.0*X + 2.0
```

This requires six multiplications and three additions.

If the polynomial is factored as follows:

```
Y = ((5.0*X + 7.0)*X + 6.0)* X + 2.0
```

evaluation requires only three multiplications and three additions. Reducing the number of multiplications reduces the execution time. For an n degree equation, the unfactored form requires

$$\sum_{i=1}^{n} i = \frac{n(n + 1)}{2}$$

multiplications, whereas the factored form requires only n multiplications.

ELIMINATING UNNECESSARY SUBPROGRAM CALLS

Subprograms are extremely useful structural components of programs. A subprogram is a block of code which is executed as a unit and which performs some part of the total processing of the program. The concept of subprograms is very general; a block of in-line statements may be considered a subprogram of the operating system under which it is executed. However, when FORTRAN programmers refer to subprograms, they usually mean FORTRAN *functions* and FORTRAN *subroutines*. Subprograms come in two flavors: *open* and *closed.*

An *open subprogram* is one which is inserted into the calling program's code every time it is invoked. Assembler language programmers frequently use open subprograms called *macro-instructions.* Open subprograms are inserted by the FORTRAN compiler for performing tasks which require only a few instructions. Functions such as FLOAT, IFIX, and ABS are frequently compiled as open subprograms.

An open subprogram is incorporated into the program's code every time it is needed.

A *closed subprogram* is one which is independent of the main routine. Closed subprograms are used more frequently than open subprograms. FORTRAN subroutines and FORTRAN functions are closed subprograms. No matter how many times it is invoked, only one copy of a closed subprogram is inserted into the program. For this reason, closed subprograms are more efficient than open subprograms in their use of processor storage. However, the code required to link a program to a subroutine and to pass it to the calling parameters imposes both a computational and a storage penalty. Thus, care should be taken to ensure efficient subprogram linkage.

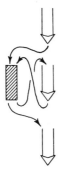

A closed subprogram is independent of its calling program and is entered by a subprogram linkage.

One of the best ways to reduce subprogram linkage overhead is to eliminate unnecessary and redundant subroutine calls. Subprograms may be invoked either *explicitly* or *implicitly*. Subroutines are explicitly invoked by means of a CALL statement, and functions are explicitly invoked by means of a function reference in an arithmetic or logical expression. Implicit invocation of a subprogram occurs when the compiler is required to insert relatively complex code into the object program. Implicit subprogram calls are generated for such things as mode conversions, subscripting, some types of exponentiation, and input/output statements. Indeed, some compilers with limited storage generate implicit calls for almost every type of statement.

Implicit Invocation

In order to reduce the number of implicit function calls, you must be aware of situations in which they are likely to be included in the object code. Visual inspection of an object listing (if available) or a "load map" may be useful here.

One situation in which implicit function calls are generated is mode conversion in an arithmetic or logical expression. The expression

$$X = A + I$$

will result in the following object code:

1. Convert the value of I to floating point, and store it in some temporary location.
2. Add the value of A to the converted value of I.
3. Store the result in X.

Some programmers explicitly recognize the fact that a conversion will be performed by writing the equivalent statement:

$$X = A + FLOAT(I)$$

However, the code generated is the same in either case. Mode conversions may be reduced by treating them as reducible expressions and assigning the conversions to temporary variables. For example, the statements

```
X1 = A + I
X2 = B + I
```

may be, more efficiently, written as

```
AI = I
X1 = A + AI
X2 = B + AI
```

It is important that you be alert to situations in which an implicit function is likely to be invoked. Sometimes a simple, innocent-looking modification to a program may allow an implicit call to sneak in. The statement

```
X = A ** 2
```

is quite straightforward but the similar statement

```
X = A ** 2.
```

will cause an implicit function call in most systems. The first statement will usually be compiled into a multiplication, whereas the second will be evaluated by logarithms.

Reducible Functions

Redundant function calls may be treated like redundant expressions and replaced by temporary variables if the function involved is reducible. A reducible function is one which keeps no history, does not perform any input or output, and does not alter any COMMON variables. A reducible function is "unaware" of its past history and leaves no trace of its having been called except by returning a single argument. When a reducible function is invoked with a particular set of arguments, it will always return the same result. Examples of reducible functions include mathematical functions such as SIN, COS, SQRT, and EXP; implicit functions such as FLOAT and IFIX; and manipulative functions such as AMAX0, AMIN0, and MOD. Irreducible functions include functions which return the time of day, functions which perform input/output, and functions which modify COMMON. A function that invokes an

sin, cos, etc. exp.

irreducible function is, thereby, irreducible. The rule for eliminating multiple occurrences of reducible functions is the same as that for redundant expressions:

> *If a reducible function is invoked more than once with identical parameters then it need be evaluated only once and its value assigned to a variable which replaces the redundant invocations of the function.*

An immediate corollary of the above rule is

> *Reducible functions may be factored in an arithmetic or logical expression.*

For example, the reducible function SIN in

$$Y = 2.0 * SIN(X) + 4.0 * SIN(X)$$

may be factored to

$$Y = 6.0 * SIN(X)$$

Less obvious, perhaps, is the possible reduction in the following expressions for rotating coordinates in a two-dimensional Cartesian plane:

```
XPRIME = X * COS(THETA) + Y * SIN(THETA)
YPRIME = X * SIN(THETA) - Y * COS(THETA)
```

which can be reduced to

```
CT = COS(THETA)
ST = SIN(THETA)
XPRIME = X * CT + Y * ST
YPRIME = X * ST - Y * CT
```

Note that the reduction will be valid no matter how many statements separate the calculation of XPRIME and YPRIME (as long as the value of THETA remains unchanged).

Many FORTRAN systems include a function for generating random numbers. If we consider RANDOM(X) to be a function which returns such a random number (X is a dummy argument), the multiple invocation of RANDOM in the statement

$$X = RANDOM(X) + RANDOM(X)$$

may not be reduced to

$$X = 2. * RANDOM(X)$$

The invocations of RANDOM will not return identical results even though the parameters are the same; hence, RANDOM is not a reducible function.

EFFICIENT SUBSCRIPTING

The data aggregates in FORTRAN are subscripted array variables — vectors and matrices. Access to an element of an array is obtained by specifying subscripts. In a one-dimensional array, for example,

$$DIMENSION \ A(10)$$

the third element is located by coding A(3), the Nth element in A(N). In two-dimensional arrays, such as

$$DIMENSION \quad B(10,10)$$

the element in the Ith row and Jth column is located by coding B(I,J). Since most computers are designed with a linear arrangement of addressable storage locations, multidimensional arrays must be mapped[2] onto a linear ordering. Thus the physical arrangement of data in the computer's storage is usually different from the logical structure of the aggregate. It is necessary to compute the address of a particular element from the subscripts given. The mappings which transform subscripts into machine addresses are called *subscripting functions*; these are inserted

---

[2] That is, a unique memory location must be associated with each element of the array. Formulas are discussed in detail later.

in the object code by the compiler. The frequent evaluation of sub-scripting functions contributes to program inefficiency, since each time reference is made to an element of an array, a physical address must be calculated.

Dimension Reduction

If a specific element of an array is to be accessed many times, it is more efficient to transfer the contents of that array location to a scalar variable. This avoids the recalculation of the address each time the value is required.

This technique can frequently save large amounts of execution time. In general, the greater the dimensionality of the array the more complex the subscripting function will be. Therefore, if you are using some cross section of an array frequently (such as the diagonal of a square matrix or one plane of a three-dimensional array), it may be more efficient to move that set of values into an array of reduced degree. Most FORTRAN compilers map two-dimensional arrays by going down the columns and across the rows from left to right. Thus, an array of three rows and three columns

A(1, 1)	A(1, 2)	A(1, 3)
A(2, 1)	A(2, 2)	A(2, 3)
A(3, 1)	A(3, 2)	A(3, 3)

would be stored as follows:

	n	n + 1	n + 2	n + 3	n + 4	n + 5	n + 6	n + 7	n + 8
location array element	(A(1, 1)	A(2, 1)	A(3, 1)	A(1, 2)	A(2, 2)	A(3, 2)	A(1, 3)	A(2, 3)	A(3, 3)

Array location (1,1) occupies the first position, (2,1) occupies the second position, (3,1) occupies the third position, (1,2) occupies the fourth position, and so on. The complete map is

```
(1, 1) ─────────────▶ 1
(2, 1) ─────────────▶ 2
(3, 1) ─────────────▶ 3
(1, 2) ─────────────▶ 4
(2, 2) ─────────────▶ 5
(3, 2) ─────────────▶ 6
(1, 3) ─────────────▶ 7
(2, 3) ─────────────▶ 8
(3, 3) ─────────────▶ 9
```

The general rule for mapping a two-dimensional array onto linear storage is

$$\text{linear position} = (J - 1) * \text{NROWS} + I$$
of location
ARRAY(I,J)

where NROWS is the number of rows in the DIMENSION statement for ARRAY. Every time an element is accessed from a two-dimensional array, the above calculation (which requires an addition, a multiplication, and a subtraction) must be performed. In some cases it may be possible to reduce the amount of subscript calculation. If the same array element is needed in several places, replace the subscripted value with a scalar variable to which the value of the element has been assigned. In the statements

```
I = K
J = K + 1
X = B(I,J) * A
Y = B(I,J) * C
Z = B(I,J) * D
```

the amount of subscripting may be reduced by coding

```
I = K
J = K + 1
TEMP = B(I,J)
X = TEMP * A
Y = TEMP * C
Z = TEMP * D
```

As with reducible expressions, some compilers will not re-subscript identical variables *provided* that the statements are immediately juxtaposed. The reason is that when new expressions are computed, they replace available values in the computer's registers. However, with most compilers, the statements

```
DIMENSION A(5,5),B(5,5)
X = A(I,J) + B(I,J)
```

will require two subscript evaluations.

Three-dimensional subscripted variables are mapped onto linear storage locations as follows: The statement

```
DIMENSION CUBE(2,3,2)
```

causes core storage to be reserved in the following order:

(1, 1, 1) ⟶	1
(2, 1, 1) ⟶	2
(1, 2, 1) ⟶	3
(2, 2, 1) ⟶	4
(1, 3, 1) ⟶	5
(2, 3, 1) ⟶	6
(1, 1, 2) ⟶	7
(2, 1, 2) ⟶	8
(1, 2, 2) ⟶	9
(2, 2, 2) ⟶	10
(1, 3, 2) ⟶	11
(2, 3, 2) ⟶	12

The leftmost subscript varies fastest; the rightmost subscript varies slowest.

The subscripting function for a three-dimensional array is

$$\text{linear position of CUBE(I,J,K)} = (K-1)*(NROWS*NLEVEL)$$
$$+ (J-1)*NLEVEL$$
$$+ I$$

where NLEVEL is the number of planes, and NROWS is the number of rows.

If a triply subscripted variable occurs at several points in a program and the subscripts do not change, they can be replaced by an unsubscripted scalar assigned the value of the subscripted element.

The "Do-It-Yourself" Technique

A substantial portion of program execution time may be spent in the calculation of the subscripting function. The elimination of some of this computation can substantially reduce the execution time. As mentioned previously, if the same subscripted element is referenced several times, some improvement may result from replacing the subscripted variable with a temporary variable assigned the value of the subscripted element. If different arrays use the same subscripts, further improvement can be obtained by performing the subscripting function in the program. Programs which involve much subscripting such as Gauss-Jordan eliminations, matrix inversions, and eigenvalue calculations can benefit from this rule.

In the following example the location to be filled is read as I, J, and K; array B receives the larger of X and Y; and array C the smaller of X and Y.

```
      DIMENSION A(8,6,40),B(8,6,40),C(8,6,40)
      DO 7 N = 1,1920
      READ(5,100) I,J,K,X,Y
100   FORMAT(3I2,2F10.2)
      A(I,J,K) = X + Y
      IF(X .GT. Y) GO TO 5
      B(I,J,K) = Y
      C(I,J,K) = X
      GO TO 7
5     B(I,J,K) = X
      C(I,J,K) = Y
7     CONTINUE
```

This program could be rewritten with a single explicit calculation of the array subscripts.

```
DIMENSION A(8,6,40),B(8,6,40),C(8,6,40)
DIMENSION AA(1920), BB(1920), CC(1920)
EQUIVALENCE ( A(1,1,1),AA(1)), (B(1,1,1),BB(1)), (C(1,1,1),CC(1))
DO 7 N=1,1920
    READ(5,100) I,J,K,X,Y
100 FORMAT (3I2, 2F10.2)
C
C     COMPUTE MSUB AS THE LINEAR SUBSCRIPT WHICH EQUALS THE SUBSCRIP
C     (I,J,K). THAT IS:
C                       A(I,J,K) IS AA(MSUB)
C                       B(I,J,K) IS BB(MSUB)
C                       C(I,J,K) IS CC(MSUB)
C
    MSUB = (K-1)*48 + (J-1)*8 + I
    AA(MSUB) = X + Y
    IF(X .GT. Y) GO TO 5
    BB(MSUB) = Y
    CC(MSUB) = X
    GO TO 7
5   BB(MSUB) = X
    CC(MSUB) = Y
7 CONTINUE
```

This technique often makes the program more difficult to understand, and special care should be taken to insert meaningful comments in the source code.

Linear Sweep

If a multidimensional array is to be accessed in a linear manner, then subscript calculations can be simplified. The multidimensional array is EQUIVALENCE'd to a one-dimensional array which can be treated in a sequential fashion. In the following example, two three-dimensional arrays are completely cleared to zero.

```
DIMENSION A(30,20,10), B(30,20,10)
DO 7 I = 1,30
DO 7 J = 1,20
DO 7 K = 1,10
A(I,J,K) = 0.0
B(I,J,K) = 0.0
7 CONTINUE
```

This program should be replaced by one which sweeps through the three-dimensional arrays in a simple sequential manner, thus. eliminating unnecessary subscript calculations.

```
    DIMENSION A(30,20,10),B(30,20,10)
    DIMENSION AA(6000),BB(6000)
    EQUIVALENCE (A(1,1,1),AA(1)), (B(1,1,1),BB(1))
    DO 7 I = 1,6000
    AA(I) = 0.0
    BB(I) = 0.0
  7 CONTINUE
```

LOOP OPTIMIZATION

In FORTRAN the most direct technique for iteration is the DO statement. Since a large proportion of the program's time is usually spent in loops, the loops should be optimized. The speed of the computer should not be abused by careless programming of loops. Operations which can be performed before entering a loop should be removed from the scope of the loop; redundant calculations should be avoided.

Removing Loop-Independent Expressions

Expressions in DO loops that involve variables which are independent of the loop variable should be evaluated outside the loop and, if necessary, stored in a temporary location. This technique avoids unnecessary and repetitive calculation. In the next example the expression $(X*X + 3.0*X + 2.0)$ is independent of the loop variable J, but will be calculated 50 times. The expression can be calculated once outside the loop and stored in location Z. Then the occurrence of the expression in the DO loop is replaced by Z:

```
    X = 3.4
    DO 9 J = 1,50
  9 Y = Y + A(J)*(X*X + 3.0*X +2.0)
```

should be replaced by

```
        X = 3.4
        Z = X*X + 3.0*X + 2.0
        DO 9 J=1,50
      9 Y = Y + A(J) * Z
```

In the following program the expression (3.0*X*SIN(X)) may be removed from the loop. As a result the expression need be evaluated only once, instead of 100 times. Notice also that the SIN function, which is reducible, is invoked only once:

```
      X = .4739
      DO 7 I = 1,100
    7 A(I) = 3.0 * X * SIN(X)
```

should be replaced by

```
      X = .4739
      Y = 3.0 * X * SIN(X)
      DO 7 I=1,100
    7 A(I) = Y
```

Expressions involving subscripted variables in which subscripts are independent of the DO loop variable should also precede the loop. This avoids the calculation of a subscripting function each time the expression is evaluated:

```
      I = K + 1
      DO 6 J = 1,30
    6 A(J) = B(J) * C(I)
```

should be replaced by

```
      I = K + 1
      TEMP = C(I)
      DO 6 J = 1,30
    6 A(J) = B(J) * TEMP
```

"Jamming"

If two adjacent DO loops have the same limits on the loop variable, it may be possible to combine the two loops. This operation not only reduces the size of the program, but can also substantially reduce the execution time.

In the following example, two 600 word arrays are set to zero by two separate DO loops:

```
      DO 20 I = 1,600
   20 A(I) = 0.0
      DO 30 I = 1,600
   30 B(I) = 0.0
```

However, only one loop is necessary:

```
      DO 40 I = 1,600
      A(I) = 0.0
   40 B(I) = 0.0
```

This technique, known as *loop jamming*, reduces overhead in the loop by 50 percent.

Unrolling

Every iteration of a DO loop requires incrementation and testing of the loop variable. This overhead may be reduced at the expense of additional instructions by the technique of "unrolling' the loop.

In the program segment

```
      DO 7 I = 1,4
    7 A(I) = 0.0
```

run time can be reduced by coding

```
      A(1) = 0.0
      A(2) = 0.0
      A(3) = 0.0
      A(4) = 0.0
```

If the number of iterations of a loop is large, a complete unrolling is impractical. The overhead may be halved by a partial unrolling as follows:

```
      DO 7 I = 1,1000
    7 A(I) = 0.0
```

may be replaced by

```
DO 7 I = 1,500
   A(I) = 0.0
7 A(I + 500) = 0.0
```

or by

```
DO 7 I = 1,999,2
   A(I) = 0.0
7 A(I + 1) = 0.0
```

If a programmer is concerned with reducing execution time, a four way unrolling is possible.

```
DO 7 I = 1,997,4
   A(I) = 0.0
   A(I + 1) = 0.0
   A(I + 2) = 0.0
7 A(I + 3) = 0.0
```

Of course, eight way, ten way, or hundred way unrollings are possible, but these are of interest only to miserly programmers, who hoard time.

Strength Reduction

Not all computer operations are performed in the same amount of time. The rule of strength reduction is that if there is a choice, the fastest operation should be used. Sometimes a slow multiplication can be replaced by a faster addition. Assume that a programmer required a variable K to be 5 times the value of the loop variable I.

```
DO 50 I = 1,5000
   K = I*5
      .
      .
      .
50 CONTINUE
```

If K were initialized to 0, he could replace the multiplication by an addition. Since the statements within the loop are executed 5000 times, the savings of execution time could add up.

```
K = 0
DO 50 I = 1,5000
K = K + 5
    •
    •
    •
50 CONTINUE
```

If the DO loop variable I were not used anywhere within the loop, an even more efficient program could be created. The variable I could be eliminated, and the DO statement could take care of the incrementation of K.

```
DO 50 K = 5,25000,5
    •
    •
    •
50 CONTINUE
```

Unswitching

If a test inside a DO loop is not influenced by any of the variables in the loop then it may be possible to remove the test from the loop. For example, in

```
DO 50 K = 1,1000
IF ( T .GT. 0.0) GO TO 40
A(K) = B(K) + C(K)
GO TO 50
40 A(K) = B(K) - C(K)
50 CONTINUE
```

the variable T is unaffected by the loop, but the IF statement is executed 1000 times. The program could be restructured to decrease the execution time by coding

```
      IF (T .GT. 0.0) GO TO 40
      DO 30 K = 1,1000
30    A(K) = B(K) + C(K)
      GO TO 60
40    DO 50 K = 1,1000
50    A(K) = B(K) - C(K)
60    CONTINUE
```

Although this second program is more complicated, the IF statement is executed only once.

EFFICIENT INITIALIZATION

The initialization statements BLOCK DATA and DATA may be used to advantage when available. Since these initialization statements preset values of previously allocated variables, they cause no increase in storage requirements. Using initialization statements benefits the program in two ways:

- The instructions and constants required for initializing the variables will be eliminated from the program reducing the size of the object program.
- The execution time of the program will be reduced because of the elimination of those statements.

Because all storage allocation in FORTRAN is "static," the data initialization statements cannot be used to initialize variables in subroutines which will be called more than once. This characteristic can be used to advantage when setting "first time"' switches and defining default values for variables.

The data initialization statements are particularly useful when arrays are being initialized. The next example shows how an initializing DO loop may be replaced by a DATA statement. Note that since no statement number precedes the DO statement, it will be executed only once. The DO is, therefore, a candidate for replacement by a DATA statement.

```
DIMENSION COST(20)
     DO 20 I = 1,20
20 COST(I) = 0.0
```

This coding may be replaced by

```
DIMENSION COST(20)
DATA COST /20 * 0.0/
```

EFFICIENT SUBROUTINE LINKAGE

When a subroutine or function is invoked, overhead is incurred in three ways:

1. linkage: The instructions required to branch to the subroutine.
2. prologue: The instructions required to initialize the subprogram. These include the saving of relevant registers and the replacement of dummy arguments by the calling parameters.
3. epilogue: The instructions required to return the subprogram's results, restore the previously saved registers, and return to the calling program.

The second and third items — prologue and epilogue — are part of the subprogram itself, whereas the first — linkage — is part of the calling program.

The simplest method of reducing linkage overhead is to invoke the subprogram as few times as necessary. This statement means that reducible functions should be reduced and redundant subroutine calls eliminated. In order to do this the techniques discussed in the first part of this chapter may be used.

When a subprogram with m parameters is invoked, the calling program passes the subroutine

> [the return address]
> [the location of the 1st parameter]
> [the location of the 2nd parameter]
> [the location of the mth parameter]

This scheme, which is used by most compilers, is called *invocation by reference*. For example, assume that variable X is stored in location 500 and the statement

$$A \ = \ COS(X)$$

is encountered. In a word-oriented machine, the object program would be

location	instruction
n	Set return to n+3
n+1	Set parameter to 500
n+2	Branch to COS
n+3	Store the result in A

The subroutine COS is unaware of where it was called from. It receives the information

$$[500]$$
$$[n+3]$$

which it interprets as

1. Get the value of location 500.
2. Compute the COSine of that value.
3. Store the COSine in some prearranged place.
4. Return to location n+3.

As you can see, adherence to pre-established conventions is vital. If, for example, the location at 500 contains an integer value, the subroutine will not know this and will produce incorrect results.

The process of transmitting the address of the argument is termed *passing the parameters.*

What must the subprogram do with parameters? Remember that the parameters with which the subroutine or function was compiled were dummy arguments. Every occurrence of a dummy argument must be replaced by the actual parameter passed. Consider the statements

$$FUNCTION \ F(X)$$
$$10 \ A \ = \ X$$

The code which would normally be generated for the statement $A = X$ is

1. Get the value of X.
2. Store it in A.

Since X is a dummy argument, however, the best that the compiler can do is to generate:

1. Get the value of **.
2. Store it in A.

The symbol ** is used to indicate an unknown address. One of the instruction sequences in the prologue will be

> Get the address which was passed
> as the argument and store it in
> ** at statement 10.

The statement will now operate correctly for this invocation of the routine.

Prologue Reduction

With many compilers, the instructions to "plug-in" the location of the subprogram parameters will be generated for *every occurrence* of the dummy variables in the subprogram. Thus, the routine

```
SUBROUTINE SUB(X)
A = X
B = X
C = X
END
```

will generate three "plug-in" sequences; this introduces both storage and computational overhead.

There are two simple solutions to this problem. The first is to copy the parameter to a variable internal to the subprogram and use the copy of the parameter. The above example could be rewritten as

```
SUBROUTINE SUB(X)
X2 = X
A = X2
B = X2
C = X2
END
```

The revised version requires two fewer "plug-ins" than the original. If the variable X is modified by the subprogram, the statement

$$X = X2$$

will cause the new value to be known to the calling routine.

This technique is only useful with scalar variables, since the overhead of copying an array is usually greater than the savings (also, the storage requirement is doubled). The formal rule is

When a parameter of a subprogram is used more than once, it may be assigned to an internal variable.

Use of COMMON

A second method of reducing the overhead of the prologue (and epilogue) is to pass as many arguments as possible via COMMON blocks. Obviously, the arguments thus passed are fixed parameters, that is, you cannot pass different parameters at different invocations.

The above subroutine might be rewritten as

```
SUBROUTINE SUB
COMMON X
    •
    •
    •
END
```

When this is done, the variable X will be known both to the subroutine and the calling program. Since COMMON variables are identified by their position in a COMMON list rather than by name, it is advisable to reserve an entire COMMON list by using named COMMON. A better way of constructing the above example would be to code

```
SUBROUTINE SUB
COMMON /SUBX/ X
  •
  •
  •
END
```

EFFICIENT I/O OPERATIONS

Even if the primary function of a program is computational, a large fraction of the execution time may be spent inputting data and outputting results. A little consideration may not only save run time but may enable the ecologically minded programmer to reduce the amount of paper needed.

If the volume of card input data is large, try to get as much data per card as possible. The fewer cards to be read, the faster the program will execute. Use a 20I4 format instead of an I4 format and thus fill the data card.

Similarly, on output, print as much per line as is consistent with legibility. The time for printing is largely a function of lines printed, not how much is on each line.

A further note for those who are environmentally oriented — get your computer center manager to set up a special bin for unwanted output. Paper companies will pay for the paper and recycle it.

Implied DO Loops

The use of the implied DO loop in an input or output list is very costly; when reading or writing an entire array it is much more efficient to use an unsubscripted array name and to omit the implied DO loop. Thus if an array were declared as

```
DIMENSION PARTNO(200)
```

the output statement

```
WRITE(6,100) (PARTNO(I), I = 1,200)
```

should be replaced by

```
WRITE(6,100) PARTNO
```

The unsubscripted array is more efficient because of the way in which most FORTRAN compilers generate instructions for I/O lists. Each data item in an I/O list causes a subroutine call at execution time. In the implied DO loop a subroutine call is performed for PARTNO(1), PARTNO(2), PARTNO(3), PARTNO(4), ... — a total of 200 subroutine calls. The suggested replacement generates only a single subroutine call and thus eliminates 199 subroutine calls — a substantial saving.

Unformatted I/O

The FORMAT statement indicates the conversions required between the external and internal representation of data. The character form of the output sent to the printer is very different from the internal form required for computation. To perform these conversions it is necessary to invoke subroutines at execution time. Because these operations often use a surprising amount of compute time, it is good practice to use unformatted I/O statements when data is written out to be re-read later by the same or another program. Information to be printed must, of course, be sent to the printer in the properly converted form.

To convert the following formatted WRITE statement

```
WRITE (8,100) NPART,NWHSE,(NSTOCK(I),I = 1,10
100 FORMAT (I10,I8,10(I6))
```

to an unformatted WRITE statement, simply delete the FORMAT number and statement:

```
WRITE(8) NPART,NWHSE,(NSTOCK(I),I = 1,10)
```

List Equivalencing

To take advantage of the efficiency provided by unsubscripted array input/output, it is often desirable to EQUIVALENCE an array to a number of variables which may be read or written as a group. This step permits the entire array to be processed by a single subroutine call. If, for example, a program were outputting five variables

```
WRITE(6,100) HOURS,WAGE,FICA,FEDTAX,STTAX
```

it would be more efficient to write

```
DIMENSION DUMMY(5)
EQUIVALENCE (HOURS,DUMMY(1)),(WAGE,DUMMY(2)),(FICA,DUMMY(3)),
1          (FEDTAX,DUMMY(4)),(STTAX,DUMMY(5))
     .
     .
     .
WRITE(6,100) DUMMY
```

This procedure would save four subroutine calls — a significant number if the WRITE statement were executed frequently.

Blocking Records

Reading or writing a record is far slower than computing. Many computers are capable of performing tens of thousands of arithmetic operations in the time that it takes to perform a single I/O operation. The disparity in time between the two types of operations exists because I/O operations are mechanical whereas arithmetic operations are electronic. In general, the process of accessing a record — starting a tape moving or positioning a disk arm — consumes the most time, the actual data transfer is rapid. Therefore we state two simple rules which may save large amounts of time by reducing the number of I/O requests:

- For recording media such as cards and print lines whose size is fixed, pack as much data per record as is consistent with legibility.
- For other recording media such as tapes and disks, write the largest records possible.

Operating systems provide a service to the programmer known as record *blocking*. Suppose you were writing card image records to a tape

```
DIMENSION NCARD(80)
WRITE (10,100) NCARD
100 FORMAT(80A1)
```

With most operating systems, it is possible to specify, on a control card, that the records are to be blocked. This means that when you execute a WRITE statement, the data will be automatically saved in the computer's memory (in a *buffer*). When a designated number of records have been accumulated, one large *block* is written on the tape or disk. The number of records accumulated before the block is written is called the *blocking factor*.

The data in the NCARD array is a single *logical record*. The illustration below shows a tape written in unblocked format, that is, with one logical record per block.

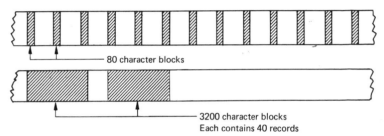

80 character blocks

3200 character blocks
Each contains 40 records

The 0.6 inch blank spaces between the blocks are called *inter-block gaps* (IBG). Notice that most of the tape is blank. With a blocking factor of 40, a larger fraction of the tape contains useful information and there is less wasted space. As a result, there are fewer tape accesses, less tape motion, and faster execution. It is important to stress that blocking has no effect on the program code — you need not be concerned with the blocking factor when writing the program. The operating system does all the work of blocking when you write and deblocking when you read. However, the larger the blocks used, the more core storage the operating system will use for buffers.

Checklist

Trimming your program

- Have you replaced redundant expressions with temporary variables?
- Have you factored polynomial expressions?
- Have you eliminated unneeded mode conversions?
- Have you used integer exponents whenever possible?
- Have you reduced function calls where possible?

Efficient subscripting
- Can you reduce the dimensions of any arrays?
- Have you stored frequently referenced locations in scalar temporaries?
- If you are accessing the array in a predetermined order, have you considered doing your own subscripting on a linear array?
- Have you EQUIVALENCE'd arrays for linear sweeps?

Loop optimization
- Have you removed all loop-independent expressions from the scope of the loops?
- If two, or more, loops have the same loop limits, have you attempted loop "jamming?"
- Can you save execution time by unrolling long loops?
- Can you replace multiplications or divisions which involve the loop index, with additions or subtractions?
- If you have IF statements within a loop which are not influenced by the loop, can you restructure by unswitching?

Initialization
- Have you employed DATA and BLOCK DATA statements for variable initialization?

Subroutine linkage
- Have you stored frequently referenced parameters in variables local to the subroutine?
- Have you used COMMON for transmitting the parameters where possible?

Input-Output
- Have you used as few print lines and punch cards as is compatible with clarity?
- Do you input and output entire arrays by using the unsubscripted name in the I/O list?
- Have you used unformatted I/O where possible?
- Do you use blocked records?
- Have you employed list equivalencing for input and output of related variables?

CHAPTER 3
REDUCING PROGRAM STORAGE REQUIREMENTS

INTRODUCTION

The storage available to a central processing unit is of two types: *processor storage* which is directly addressable and *auxiliary storage* which is not directly addressable. Program instructions which reside on auxiliary storage devices must be transferred to processor storage before they can be executed. Similarly, data on auxiliary storage devices must be accessed and placed in processor storage prior to use.

The advantages of each of the two storage classes are related to their design. Processor storage has a short access time but is expensive since ferrite cores, rods, or monolithic circuits are used. Auxiliary storage devices such as magnetic tape drives, disk drives, drums, data cell drives, or some types of "bulk core storage" are slower but less expensive. Information that is voluminous or must be kept for long periods is stored on auxiliary storage media and is brought into the processor storage when needed. Frequently the auxiliary storage media can be kept at a location remote from the computer and mounted on an appropriate device when needed.

The high cost of processor storage dictates that a good program should use as little processor storage as is necessary for efficient execution. This is particularly important in a multi-programmed environment where processor storage saved may be used by other programs, thus improving overall utilization of the computer. Decreasing the storage requirement of a program is accomplished by reducing the number of instructions in the program and reducing the space required for the data. Unfortunately, the goal of minimizing processor storage utilization is not always compatible with attempts at minimizing compute time. Data which is efficiently packed in processor storage or stored on auxiliary devices may be less easily accessible than data which is stored in a more convenient, but less compact, way. The program designer bears the responsibility of deciding how much compute time and voluntary wait time he is willing to sacrifice for a reduction in the processor storage requirement.

The guidelines are clear. The program should have as few instructions as possible. Redundant code should be eliminated, and efficient algorithms with as few steps as possible should be used. In programs which manipulate large volumes of data, effort should be applied to eliminate redundant data. The remaining data should be stored in a compact form. Finally, both programs and data may be temporarily saved on auxiliary storage devices in order to liberate areas of processor storage.

ELIMINATING UNNECESSARY INSTRUCTIONS

A good program does exactly what is required and no more. Unnecessary operations and redundant statements are useless and should be eliminated. Reduction of the number of operations in a program will result in a reduction of the amount of storage needed to contain that program and, frequently, a reduction in run time.

Programs may be shortened by eliminating unnecessary initializations. If a value of a variable is established by an input statement, there is no need to clear the location. In the first example, it is unnecessary to initialize X, I, J, and K to zero, since their values will be established by the READ statement before the values are referenced. Thus, the program fragment

```
I = 0
J = 0
K = 0
READ (1,100)I,J,K,L
L = 4.3 * X + I - J * K
```

should be rewritten as

```
READ (1,100)I,J,K
L = 4.3 * X + I - J * K
```

By eliminating the four unnecessary initializations to zero, both space and time are saved without affecting the program's results.

Resetting

If the value of a variable is initially established by an assignment statement (before it is referenced on the right side of an assignment statement), there is no need to clear the location. Thus, the program

```
    ISUM = 0
    DO 25 I = 1,50
    II = 0
    ROOTI = 0.0
    II = I * I
    ROOTI = SQRT(FLOAT(I))
    ISUM = ISUM + I
 25 WRITE (3,300) I,II,ROOTI,ISUM
300 FORMAT (' ',2I12,F12.4,I12)
    CALL EXIT
    END
```

may be reduced to

```
    ISUM = 0
    DO 25 I = 1,50
    II = I*I
    ROOTI = SQRT(FLOAT(I))
    ISUM = ISUM + I
 25 WRITE (3,300) I,II,ROOTI,ISUM
300 FORMAT (' ',2I12,F12.4,I12)
    CALL EXIT
    END
```

It is unnecessary to initialize II or ROOTI to zero, since their values are not referenced on the right side of an assignment statement before being set. However, ISUM must be initialized, since it is referenced on the right side of the statement before statement 25.

Setting Data Values

If the value of a variable is known prior to execution, the value should be set by a DATA statement rather than by an assignment statement. Thus if π and e are needed, the assignment statements

```
PI = 3.14159
E  = 2.71828
```

should not be used. Instead the following DATA statement is preferred:

```
DATA PI,E /3.14159,2.71828/
```

Similarly, if a calendar program needs a table of the numerical day of the year of the beginning of each month, then

```
DIMENSION NCLNDR(12)
NCLNDR(1)  =    1
NCLNDR(2)  =   32
NCLNDR(3)  =   60
NCLNDR(4)  =   91
NCLNDR(5)  =  121
NCLNDR(6)  =  152
NCLNDR(7)  =  182
NCLNDR(8)  =  213
NCLNDR(9)  =  244
NCLNDR(10) =  274
NCLNDR(11) =  305
NCLNDR(12) =  335
```

should be replaced by

```
DIMENSION NCLNDR(12)
DATA NCLNDR /1,32,60,91,121,152,182,213,244,274,305,335/
```

This DATA statement replaces twelve assignment statements and frees the storage space that would be required for those instructions. Compute time will be reduced as well.

In the preceding four examples, assignment statements have been eliminated without changing the results of the programs and the programs take less storage and time. These techniques are recommended programming rules but they will rarely yield more than a few hundred locations.

Function Calls

A more beneficial technique is to eliminate calls to in-line (open) functions. An in-line function is one which is inserted in the program by the compiler every time the function is used; thus multiple copies of the function are kept in storage. This differs from a closed subroutine or external function which is stored only once. Each mixed mode expression causes a copy of the code which converts data types to be inserted into the program. Library routines such as those that do mode conversion (FLOAT, SNGL, DBL), calculate absolute values (ABS), truncate (IFIX), find the largest or smallest values of a group of variables (AMAX, AMIN), or do remaindering (MOD) are usually in-line functions. The user should check the language or programmer's manual for particular dialects of FORTRAN to determine which functions are inserted in-line. Minimizing the number of calls to in-line functions will reduce the length of the program. Thus,

```
Y = SQRT(FLOAT(N)) + SQRT(FLOAT(N) + 1.0)
```

requires two copies of the FLOAT function. If the program is modified to

```
XN = N
Y = SQRT(XN) + SQRT(XN + 1.0)
```

the floating point conversion is done once implicitly in the first statement and only one copy of that routine is needed. Similarly,

```
X = AMAX0(A,B,C,D)
Y = AMAX0(A,B,C,D)
```

should be replaced by

```
X  =  AMAXO(A,B,C,D)
Y  =  X
```

These rules will reduce the storage used and will decrease compute time.

USING OVERLAYS

A frequent problem in programming is that the computer's main storage is not able to contain the entire program. There is a corollary to Murphy's law[1] which states that "programs expand to exceed the available memory." When a program cannot fit into the available main storage, it is necessary to store parts of the program on secondary storage (disks and drums) and transfer the program segments to main storage as they are needed. The segments transferred to main storage will overlay some of the segments already in main storage; therefore this process is known as *overlaying*. Overlaying may be accomplished in two ways: *virtual memory overlays* and *planned overlays*. Virtual memory overlays are available only on computers with very sophisticated operating systems. In a virtual memory overlay, the program is arbitrarily divided into fixed length segments (*pages*) by the operating system. These pages are then automatically transferred by the operating system to main storage as required. Virtual memory overlays are very convenient for the programmer since they are totally automatic; unfortunately very few computers provide this service to the programmer.

Far more common is the planned overlay. In a planned overlay, the programmer is responsible for designating the segments to be transferred to main storage; the operating system performs the actual loading of the segment. Programs are naturally structured into subprograms, which serve as the units of transfer. That is, the smallest program segment which can be transferred to main storage at any time is a subprogram.

[1] Murphy's law states that "if anything can go wrong, it will."

A small fraction of the program, called the *main overlay* or *root phase*, must remain in the processor storage throughout execution in order to call in the appropriate overlays or phrases. At the start of execution, the processor storage could be represented as

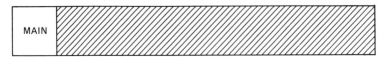

After one overlay is brought in, the processor storage contains

After some computations are performed in OVERLAY 1, a second overlay might completely replace the first:

A third and fourth overlay could be then brought in:

And finally, a fifth overlay might replace the fourth one:

In order to accomplish planned overlay, it is necessary to inform the operating system of the overlay structure. This is usually done quite simply by means of control cards. Since the details vary considerably among various computers, the appropriate programming manual should be consulted for specific details. Perhaps the most common error is to forget that when a segment is overlayed the values stored in the data areas of the subprograms are lost. Therefore, care must be taken to ensure that you don't attempt to save data between successive entrances to a subprogram. For example, subroutine

```
SUBROUTINE KOUNT
DATA KVAL /0/
KVAL = KVAL + 1
WRITE(6,100) KVAL
        •
        •
        •
RETURN
END
```

would cause problems (in most systems) if it were overlayed and then reloaded since KVAL would be initialized to 0 each time. The usual technique, in these cases, is to place this type of data in COMMON areas which then become part of the root segment and are never overlayed.

ELIMINATING UNUSED DATA SPACE

Equivalence

The most obvious area for reducing the storage required is in the organization of data stored in arrays. A useful technique is to force two or more data arrays to share the same space in storage. For example, if A, a 500 element one-dimensional array, is used in one part of a program and B, another array of 500 elements (or less), is needed in another portion of the program, they can be forced to share the same storage locations by including an EQUIVALENCE statement after the DIMENSION statements. For example,

```
DIMENSION A(500),B(500)
EQUIVALENCE ( A(1),B(1) )
```

A(1) or B(1)	A(2) or B(2)	A(3) or B(3)	A(4) or B(4)		A(499) or B(499)	A(500) or B(500)

which causes A(1) and B(1), A(2) and B(2), ... to share the same locations. Be careful to double check that the two arrays are never used at the same time. The situation is analogous to two people who want to use a locker like those found in bus or train stations; both cannot use it at the same time.

Arrays of different dimensions may be EQUIVALENCE'd. If a two-dimensional array were used in the first half of a program and a one-dimensional array were needed for an independent section of the program, the following statements might be used:

```
DIMENSION A(50,50),B(2500)
EQUIVALENCE ( A(1,1),B(1) )
```

A(1,1)	A(2,1)	A(3,1)	A(4,1)	
B(1)	B(2)	B(3)	B(4)	

A(1,2)	A(2,2)	A(3,2)	A(4,2)	
B(51)	B(52)	B(53)	B(54)	

A(1,50)	A(2,50)	A(3,50)		A(48,50)	A(49,50)	A(50,50)
B(2451)	B(2452)	B(2453)		B(2498)	B(2499)	B(2500)

The A array and the B array share the same location.

The use of EQUIVALENCE eliminates wasted space. When one array's space is no longer needed, it can be used by another array.

Occasionally, it may be useful to have two copies of the same data in storage — one copy INTEGER and the other REAL. If sufficient storage is not available, one copy can be stored and the mode can be changed in place when required. Assume the array of 1600 elements is referred to as I when INTEGER and AI when REAL. Then it is possible to write

```
DIMENSION I(1000),AI(1000)
EQUIVALENCE ( I(1),AI(1) )
```

causing the two arrays to be in the same storage locations. If the data is to be converted from INTEGER to REAL, the following statements are executed:

```
      DO 50 J = 1,1000
   50 AI(J) = I(J)
```

To convert back to INTEGER,

```
      DO 60 J = 1,1000
   60 I(J) = AI(J)
```

Of course this conversion process is time consuming, but only one copy of the data is kept in storage.

Irregularly Shaped Data Structures

Because FORTRAN is limited to defining rectangular arrays, storage space may be wasted when other forms are needed. Occasionally lower triangular (or upper triangular) arrays are needed but a square array must be defined. Consider the lower triangular array TRIANG:

DIMENSION TRIANG(8,8)

a_{11}	—	—	—	—	—	—	—
a_{21}	a_{22}	—	—	—	—	—	—
a_{31}	a_{32}	a_{33}	—	—	—	—	—
a_{41}	a_{42}	a_{43}	a_{44}	—	—	—	—
a_{51}	a_{52}	a_{53}	a_{54}	a_{55}	—	—	—
a_{61}	a_{62}	a_{63}	a_{64}	a_{65}	a_{66}	—	—
a_{71}	a_{72}	a_{73}	a_{74}	a_{75}	a_{76}	a_{77}	—
a_{81}	a_{82}	a_{83}	a_{84}	a_{85}	a_{86}	a_{87}	a_{88}

In this case an 8 by 8 array has been reserved but only 36 out of 64 or just over 50 percent of the locations are used. For a triangular array of n rows only $n(n + 1)/2$ locations are needed. A one-dimensional array of the proper length should be allocated and the user should do the mapping onto a triangle array:

I, J	K
(1, 1)	1
(2, 1)	2
(2, 2)	3
(3, 1)	4
(3, 2)	5
(3, 3)	6
(4, 1)	7
(4, 2)	8
⋮	
(8, 7)	35
(8, 8)	36

Thus TRIANG should be DIMENSION'ed TRIANG(36).

If the (I,J) position is required,

$$K = I * (I-1)/2 + J$$

and TRIANG(K) should be referred to.

This concept may also be used with symmetric matrices. A matrix is symmetric if the lower triangular part matches the upper triangular part. More formally, a matrix A is symmetric if the transpose of A equals A, that is $A(I,J) = A(J,I)$. For symmetric matrices only the lower triangular (or upper triangular) portion need be stored; if a reference is made to the upper triangular section, it must be converted into a reference to the lower triangular part. For an 8 by 8 symmetric array, we need a 36 element one-dimensional array.

```
DIMENSION SYMMET(36)
```

If the (I,J) element is needed, we must check to see if it is in the upper triangle and make the transformation, when necessary.

```
      IF (J .GT. I) GO TO 70
      II = I
      JJ = J
      GO TO 80
70    II = J
      JJ = I
80    K = II * (II-1)/2 + JJ
```

and SYMMET(K) should be referred to. It should be clear that if only the diagonal of a matrix is needed, the diagonal elements should be stored in a one-dimensional array. For an n by n array A, the diagonal elements should be stored in a one-dimensional array ADIAG of n elements. A reference to A(I,I) would become a reference to ADIAG(I).

For block diagonal arrays such as

$$
\begin{matrix}
a_{11} & a_{12} & - & - & - & - & - \\
a_{21} & a_{22} & a_{23} & - & - & - & - \\
- & a_{32} & a_{33} & a_{34} & - & - & - \\
- & - & a_{43} & a_{44} & a_{45} & - & - \\
- & - & - & a_{54} & a_{55} & a_{56} & - \\
- & - & - & - & \cdot & \cdot & \cdot \\
& & & & \cdot & \cdot & \cdot \\
& & & & & \cdot & \cdot & \cdot
\end{matrix}
$$

$$
\begin{matrix}
a_{n-1,n-2} & a_{n-1,n-1} & a_{n-1,n} \\
& a_{n,n-1} & a_{n,n}
\end{matrix}
$$

a mapping should be created to allow the storage of the useful elements in a one-dimensional array.

These mapping rules will eliminate wasting unused locations at the expense of increased compute time.

Repeated Array Elements

There may be rectangular or square matrices in which many rows contain the same elements and will never have differing elements. Only one copy of that row should be stored, and a table should be kept to indicate where that copy is kept. For example, in the array DIMENSION'ed IDATA(10,5):

```
4 8 7 9 7
7 7 8 4 0
9 8 6 5 3
4 8 7 9 7
9 8 6 5 3
1 4 2 0 2
4 8 7 9 7
7 7 8 4 0
9 8 6 5 3
4 8 7 9 7
```

rows 1, 4, 7, and 10 are identical; as are rows 2 and 8; and rows 3, 5, and 9.

We need store only the array DIMENSION'ed NDATA(4,5)

$$
\begin{array}{ccccc}
4 & 8 & 7 & 9 & 7 \\
7 & 7 & 8 & 4 & 0 \\
9 & 8 & 6 & 5 & 3 \\
1 & 4 & 2 & 0 & 2
\end{array}
$$

and a one-dimensional array NTABLE(10) containing

$$
\begin{array}{c}
1 \\
2 \\
3 \\
1 \\
3 \\
4 \\
1 \\
2 \\
3 \\
1
\end{array}
$$

which points to the appropriate row of the NDATA array.

If the (I,J) element of the IDATA array is needed, set

$$
K = NTABLE(I)
$$

and retrieve NDATA(K,J).

The amount of storage freed by this method is a function of the frequency of repetition of rows. It should be clear that the extra access to look in NTABLE will cause the program to run more slowly. A similar technique could be employed if an array has many identical columns.

Sparse Matrices

In economic analysis, in solving partial differential equations, and in other situations, only a small fraction of the elements of an array have nonzero values. For example,

$$
\begin{array}{cccccc}
0.0 & 4.0 & 0.0 & 0.0 & 0.0 & 0.0 \\
1.0 & 0.0 & 0.0 & 0.0 & 1.0 & 0.0 \\
0.0 & 0.0 & 1.0 & 0.0 & 0.0 & 0.0 \\
0.0 & 0.0 & 0.0 & 1.0 & 0.0 & 0.0 \\
0.0 & 3.0 & 0.0 & 0.0 & 0.0 & 0.0 \\
0.0 & 0.0 & 0.0 & 0.0 & 0.0 & 2.0 \\
\end{array}
$$

Such arrays are called sparse matrices and may be stored in more efficient ways. In solving partial differential equations, only 3 or 4 percent of the locations may be needed in a 100 by 100 array. Even though the alternate storage technique may be complicated, the payoff in freed storage locations can be substantial.

Although many techniques are used, we present the most intuitively obviously one: Store the row and column position and the value of the nonzero elements. Thus, we have three one-dimensional arrays, NROW, NCOL, and VALUE.

NROW	NCOL	VALUE
1	2	4.0
2	1	1.0
2	4	1.0
3	3	1.0
4	4	1.0
5	2	3.0
6	6	2.0

To access any element of the array, search through the table of rows and columns till the required row and column is found and return the value. If the required row and column is not in the list, the value 0.0 is returned. The technique takes time to execute, but the savings in storage can be worthwhile. Since three locations are needed for each nonzero element, this method is useful only if less than one-third of the locations are nonzero.

```
C      THIS FUNCTION IS CALLED BY THE USER AS FOLLOWS:
C
C        V = SPARSE(I,J)
C
C      IF THE CELL 'I,J' HAS A NON-ZERO VALUE, THE ROUTINE
C      RETURNS THE VALUE, OTHERWISE IT RETURNS 0.0
C      THUS THE MAIN PROGRAM THINKS THAT SPARSE IS A
C      BIG MATRIX YET WE HAVE ONLY RESERVED 500 LOCATIONS.
C
C      ALSO NOTE THAT SINCE A FUNCTION CALL LOOKS LIKE A
C      MATRIX REFERENCE 'SPARSE' MAY BE USED EXACTLY AS
C      THOUGH IT WERE DIMENSIONED IN THE MAIN PROGRAM.
C      FOR EXAMPLE:
C
C        X = SPARSE(I,J) + 2.0 * SPARSE(M,N)
C
C      OF COURSE, SPARSE MAY NOT BE USED ON THE LEFT-HAND
C      SIDE OF AN ARITHMETIC EXPRESSION
C
C      FOR THIS EXAMPLE, ASSUME THAT THE VALUES WERE
C      PLACED IN THE SPARSE MATRIX BY ANOTHER PROGRAM ...
C
       FUNCTION SPARSE(I,J)
       COMMON /SP/ N,NROW(500),NCOL(500),VALUE(500)
       DO 10 K = 1,N
       IF (NROW(K).NE.I .OR. NCOL(K).NE.J) GO TO 10
       SPARSE = VALUE(K)
       GO TO 999
  10   CONTINUE
       SPARSE = 0.0
 999   RETURN
       END
```

REDUCING STORAGE NEEDED FOR I/O OPERATIONS

Buffering

In some programming systems, you can control the blocking factor and the amount of buffer space used for input/output operations. Blocking of records is the term used to describe the process in which several logical records are accumulated in processor storage and then are written out as a single physical block. The result is that fewer I/O operations are required, and better use is made of the output media. If a blocking factor of 10 is indicated, the results of ten WRITE statements are kept in processor storage. After the tenth WRITE statement, all ten records are output. On input, groups of ten records are read in and passed to the user program one record at a time as READ statements are executed. The space in which the groups of records are stored is called the buffer. Double buffering refers to the technique of having two buffers available so that while one buffer is being read or written, the other can be filled. Both of these techniques speed up programs which perform large amounts of I/O, but a great deal of processor storage space must be reserved for buffers. If you are more concerned with saving space than time, buffer allocations should be reduced.

DATA COMPACTION

Binary Packing

Often, a large volume of binary information, such as the results of a true-false examination or a yes-no questionnaire, must be stored. For example, we might ask 20 people to answer the following question:

Question (Q1) What is your sex? [ ] male   [ ] female

The 20 answers could be stored in 20 separate words. A zero could represent male and a 1 could represent female. However, this would be wasteful. A more efficient technique is to store all 20 responses in a single word. The results might appear as

01100111110010101110

There might be a second question such as

Question (Q2) How old are you? [ ] under 21   [ ] over 21

Again, let 0 indicate under 21 and 1 represent over 21. The 20 answers could be stored as

11110001010101100001

The 40 responses are contained in two words of storage rather than in 40 words of storage.

The most common operations on binary data are *and, or, exclusive or,* and *not.* Suppose we had two four-bit logical words A=1100 and B=1010, then

	A 1100		A 1100		A 1100
and B	1010	*or* B	1010	*exclusive or* B	1010
	1000		1110		0110

The *not* operation has only one operand and simply changes every 0 to a 1 and every 1 to a 0. Thus,

$$not \text{ A is } 0011 \quad \text{and} \quad not \text{ B is } 0101$$

Going back to our two questions, if we were looking for females, we would simply scan the word containing the answers to Question (1). Every position that has a 1 in it represents a female. From the right, the second, third, fourth, sixth, eighth, etc. persons are female. To search for males, scan for 0's, or apply the *not* operation and search for 1's. To find people who are both female and under 21, we *and* the two sets of responses and search for 1's.

Question (Q1)	01100111110010101110
Question (Q2)	11110001010101100001
(Q1) *and* (Q2)	01100001010000100000

There are five females under 21 in our group of 20.

Another search might be for a female *or* anyone who is over 21.

Question (Q1)	01100111110010101110
Question (Q2)	11110001010101100001
(Q1) *or* (Q2)	11110111110111101111

There are 17 people in our group of 20 who fit these qualifications.

Combinations of the logical operations are sometimes useful. A search for females under 21 would require (Q1) *and* (*not*(Q2)). With other variables more complicated cases can be contrived.

Some versions of FORTRAN have operators which allow for binary bit strings. If not, then assembly language subroutines can be used. A less efficient technique is to try to duplicate the assembly language operations in FORTRAN. The binary bit string should be loaded into an integer location. To test if the rightmost bit is 0 or 1 is equivalent to testing for evenness or oddness of an integer word. The second bit from the right can be examined by dividing by 2^1 and then testing for even-odd. The third bit from the right is tested by dividing by 2^2 and then checking for even-odd. Division by 2^n is equivalent to shifting right by n bits. Multiplication by 2^n accomplishes a left shift of n bits. Care must be taken of the sign bit and of the possibility of overflow. It should also be noted that shifting by division or multiplication destroys some of the bits. This makes it wise to copy the original bit string before doing any testing. To change a 0 to a 1 in the nth bit from the rightmost bit add 2^n. To change a 1 to a 0 subtract the same power of two. Although these procedures are tricky in FORTRAN, the savings of storage space are often worthwhile.

Creating binary bit strings makes efficient use of storage space which is expensive and usually limited.

Decimal Packing

Binary packing, as explained in the previous section, is usually simple when done in assembly language, but is more difficult for the high-level language user. If 16-bit quantities are to be stored in a 32-bit machine, it should be possible to pack two 16-bit numbers in a 32-bit word. Some machines have half-word operations to make this process straightforward. Certain FORTRAN or other high-level language compilers allow the user to define half-word integer quantities by writing INTEGER*2.

Decimal packing schemes are easier than binary packing techniques in FORTRAN when integer mode is used. For example, four examination scores ranging from 00 to 99 are to be stored per student. We should be able to store all four scores (96, 87, 82, 91) in one rather than four words of storage. Load in

the first score	96
multiply by 100	9600
add the second score	9687
multiply by 100	968700
add the third score	968782
multiply by 100	96878200
add the fourth score	96878291

Assume that the marks are in a location called ITEST. To access the fourth score take MOD (ITEST, 100). Recall that the MOD function takes the remainder of the first argument after division by the second argument. The second score is obtained by MOD (ITEST/ 10000, 100). (Dividing ITEST by 10000 leaves 9687. The remainder of 9687 after division by 100 is 87, the second score.) The first score is MOD(ITEST/1000000, 100) or ITEST/1000000.

When using decimal packing, the largest decimal number that may be stored in an integer location must never be exceeded. Overflow would result and information would be destroyed.

Prime Factor Packing

Prime factor packing is another technique that is sometimes used to save storage. A prime number is assigned for each of several binary choices. The product of all the primes of the choices selected is stored. As an example, assume that we are trying to determine preference in foreign foods. We assign Chinese, 2; French, 3; Italian, 5; and Indian, 7. For someone who likes Chinese, Italian, and Indian, we assign a value of 2*5*7=70. A person who likes only French and Italian would get a composite code of 3*5=15. There is a unique number for all combinations. To find out if a person likes or dislikes a certain type of food, we determine whether the corresponding prime number is a factor of the composite code. Thus, 15 is exactly divisible by 3 and 5 indicating a preference for French and Italian foods. This method is clever, but not as efficient as binary packing.

There may also be special techniques which are dependent on the particular types of data being used. For example, in a medical study, a man's weight in pounds might be stored as a positive floating point number and a woman's weight as a negative floating point number. This avoids the need to have a separate field to indicate sex.

Checklist

Unneeded instructions
- Have you eliminated useless statements?
- Have you optimized arithmetic expressions according to the rules presented in Chapter 2?

- Do you avoid initializing variables that are reset before their value is referenced?
- Have you used DATA statements for initialization?
- Have you avoided unneeded function calls? Especially to in-line functions?

Overlays
- Have you considered overlay for large programs?
- Have you modularized your program so that it could be overlayed if needed?

Compacting data
- Have you reused storage where possible by equivalencing variables to each other?
- Have you created efficient array structures to eliminate unused locations?
- Do you store sparse matrices as vectors with pointers to the elements?
- Do you use one of the packing techniques mentioned in this chapter for small data items?

CHAPTER 4

INCREASING COMPUTATIONAL ACCURACY

INTRODUCTION

Even computers make mistakes. Although it is extremely rare for a computer to make arithmetic errors such as adding two and two and getting five or to make operational errors such as adding when multiplication was programmed, more subtle errors often occur. These mistakes do not mean that computers are undependable or that we must check all computer calculations by hand; they do mean that care should be taken in writing programs in order to prevent the occurrence of computational inaccuracy.

Inaccuracy results from the way in which computers store and manipulate numbers. Our mathematical training tells us that

$$(1./3.)*3.$$

is precisely and incontestably 1 but a computer is likely to disagree. The result of dividing 1. by 3. is the infinitely repeating decimal .333333333... which cannot be accurately represented in the hardware of a finite computer. When .333333333... is multiplied by 3. the result is a bit less than 1. The difference may seem minute, but the compounding of these minor faults by millions of operations can produce major errors and invalidate the results.

As programmers, we would like to produce correct mathematical answers. An understanding of the internal representation and manipulation of numbers can help us to guarantee the accuracy of our results.

INTEGER ARITHMETIC

Internal Representation and Truncation

FORTRAN INTEGERs are always whole numbers and are represented internally as binary numbers. For example, the decimal integer 13

$$13 = 1 \times 10^1 + 3 \times 10^0 = 10 + 3$$

may be stored in a computer as

$$1101 = 1*2^3 + 1*2^2 + 0*2^1 + 1*2^0 = 8+4+0+1 = 13$$

Since every whole decimal number can be written as a binary number, there is no error in the internal representation of a FORTRAN INTEGER. Additions, subtractions, and multiplications are performed precisely as we would expect as long as the quantities are in the range of permissible values.

Division can cause difficulty since, for example, dividing the integer 5 by the integer 2 yields 2.5 which is not an integer. An algebraist would point out that the integers are closed under the operations of addition, multiplication, and subtraction, but not under the operation of division. The problem of what to do with the fractional part is resolved by simply eliminating it. The process is called truncation rounding. Thus,

$$\frac{7}{2} = 3 \qquad \frac{9}{4} = 2 \qquad \frac{9}{5} = 1 \qquad \frac{199}{50} = 3 \text{ (not 4)}$$

If a computer were calculating student test averages with

```
MARK1 = 89
MARK2 = 90
MARK3 = 90
NAVG  = (MARK1 + MARK2 + MARK3)/3
```

NAVG would be 89 and the student might receive a B instead of an A. To accomplish *symmetric rounding* (round down if the fraction is less than 0.5 and round up if the fraction is greater than or equal to 0.5), the division may be performed in REAL mode with 0.5 added to the quotient before truncating back to an INTEGER. The statement to calculate the average should be

```
NAVG = FLOAT(MARK1 + MARK2 + MARK3)/3.0 + 0.5
```

The result of the division is 89.66666; with the addition of 0.5 we get 90.1666, which is truncated to 90 when it is stored in the INTEGER location NAVG.

Overflow

The range of permissible INTEGER values is determined by the number of binary digits (bits) available in a memory word. This varies from computer to computer: The IBM 360/370 series has a 32-bit word and can store integers ranging from -2147483647 to 2147483647.

If a computation inadvertently exceeds the representable range, a condition known as *overflow* occurs and results will not be correct. The programmer may not even be aware of the error. The greatest danger comes in multiplication of large values and in repeated additions/subtractions. Thus, an innocent-looking function to calculate the factorial of the input argument

```
      FUNCTION NFACT(N)
      NFACT = 1
      IF (N .LT. 2) GO TO 15
      DO 10 I = 2,N
   10 NFACT = NFACT * I
   15 RETURN
      END
```

will not be correct if run on an IBM 360/370 with N greater than 12.

Under some operating systems it is possible to determine if overflow has occurred by calling certain system subroutines. Special software packages are available which use several words to store a value and simulate extended precision arithmetic operations.

REAL NUMBERS

Internal Representation

Scientists often use a notation in which numbers are represented by a *mantissa* (*fraction*) and *characteristic* (*exponent*). For example, the number 546.0 may be represented as $.546 \times 10^3$. The characteristic is $+3$ and the mantissa is .546. Similarly,

96840000	−789	.00046	−.0000049
$.9684 \times 10^8$	$-.789 \times 10^3$	$.46 \times 10^{-3}$	$-.49 \times 10^{-5}$

The characteristic indicates how many places, and in which direction, the decimal point has been moved. A negative characteristic means that the decimal point has been shifted to the right, and a positive characteristic indicates that the decimal point has been shifted to the left. Computers use a similar system for representing REAL numbers. Binary numbers can be separated into a characteristic and mantissa. The decimal number 12 is 1100.0000 in binary and could be represented by 0.1100 as the mantissa and 100 as the characteristic, indicating that the binary point has been shifted four places to the left. The decimal number 12.25 is 1100.0100. Each place to the right of the decimal point indicates increasing negative powers of 2. Thus, 1100.0110

$$1*2^3 + 1*2^2 + 0*2^1 + 0*2^0 + 0*2^{-1} + 1*2^{-2} + 1*2^{-3} + 0*2^{-4}$$

$$= 8 + 4 + 0 + 0 + 0 + .250 + .125 + .000$$

$$= 12.375$$

The mantissa of this number is .11000110 and the characteristic is 100 indicating that the binary point has been shifted to the left and that to restore the number to its original form, the binary point must be shifted four places to the right.

Other examples of binary fractions are

11.5	23.625	.0625
1011.1000	00010111.1010	.0001

The IBM 360/370 stores binary floating point numbers in 32-bit words. The leftmost bit is the sign of the fraction, 0 for plus and 1 for minus. The next seven bits store the characteristic, and the rightmost 24 bits hold the binary mantissa. Since the System/360 is a hexadecimal machine, the characteristic indicates how many groups of four bits the binary point should be shifted from its starting point between the eighth and ninth bits from the left.

0	0000000	.	000000000000000000000000
	⟵ ⟶	↑	⟵——— 24 bits ———⟶
sign	7 bits	implied	mantissa
	characteristics	binary	
		point	

A binary characteristic of 1000000 (decimal 64) means no shifting, i.e., the binary point follows the characteristic and remains between the eighth and ninth bits from the left. A characteristic of 1000001 (decimal 65) indicates that the binary point should be shifted 1 hexadecimal digit (4 bits) to the right. That would move the binary point to between the twelfth and thirteenth bits from the left. 1000010 (decimal 66) indicates a right shift of 2 hexadecimal digits (8 bits); a left shift of 1 hexadecimal digit is described by a characteristic of 0111111 (decimal 63).

Thus, the decimal number +5. which is 101 as a binary integer is stored in binary floating point as

0	1000001	0101 0000 0000 0000 0000 0000
sign	characteristic	mantissa

Remember, the characteristic 1000001 indicates that the binary point is to be shifted one hexadecimal digit or four bits to the right. A characteristic of 1000011 would indicate that the binary point is 3 hexadecimal digits or 12 bits to the right. That would be

0101 0000 0000.0000 0000 0000

or 1280 decimal. The decimal value .625 is 0.101 or in floating point notation.

0 1000000 10100000000000000000000

Other examples are

15	−15
0 1000001 11110000000000000000000	1 1000001 11110000000000000000000
1.25	−1.75
0 1000001 00010100000000000000000	1 1000001 00011100000000000000000

The conversion from decimal to binary floating point is difficult, but the FORTRAN user can rest content knowing that the conversion routines are part of the compiler and do not require his attention.

In DOUBLE PRECISION two 32-bit words are used to store the information. This means that 56 bits are used for the fraction giving far greater accuracy. Single precision REAL numbers have approximately 7.2 decimal places of accuracy, whereas DOUBLE PRECISION has 14 or 15 decimal places. In either case, the characteristic is the same length, 7 bits. The absolute size of numbers that can be stored is the same, only the accuracy is increased with double precision. Similar schemes are used in other computers, and the manufacturer's manual should be consulted.

The finite number of bits per word implies that there must be a maximum size for the exponent and that the fractional part will not be able to represent every number accurately. Certainly infinitely repeating decimals such as .1666666... must be rounded off in order to be stored internally. Secondly, unlike whole numbers, not all decimal fractions can be represented precisely in binary. This second case produces an undesirable result when an IBM 360/370 (which has a 24-bit mantissa) is used to run this program:

```
      N = 1.2 * 10.0
      WRITE(3,101) N
  101 FORMAT (' THE VALUE OF N IS',I3)
      CALL EXIT
      END
THE VALUE OF N IS 11
```

The number 1.2 cannot be represented precisely, and when the internal binary value is multiplied by 10.0 the product is slightly less than 12. When the result is stored in the integer location N, truncation rounding is performed and the value of N is 11.

Having accepted this disturbing result, you might expect that if you wrote

```
     N = 1.5 * 10.0
     WRITE(3,101) N
 101 FORMAT (' THE VALUE OF N IS',I3)
     CALL EXIT
     END
```

the value of N would be 14, but you would be wrong. In this case, 1.5 can be represented precisely internally as a binary fraction and when we multiply by 10.0 the result is accurate since no truncation rounding has occurred.

The point of these exercises is that not all decimal numbers can be stored precisely in a finite word length machine and that care must be taken when dealing with real numbers. The most common trap that novice programmers fall into is attempting to compare a calculated REAL value and a specified REAL value for equality. For example, if values for A and B were calculated and we had

```
     C = A * B
     IF ( C .EQ. 7.4 ) GO TO 45
```

it would take extreme luck to satisfy the test. *Do not* test for equality of real values, instead test if you are within some error distance from the desired result:

```
C = A * B
IF (ABS(C - 7.4) .LT. .00001) GO TO 45
```

REAL ARITHMETIC

Addition or Subtraction of Widely Differing Values

Doing arithmetic on finite word length machines can be tricky if the operands are sufficiently different in size. Consider the following program:

```
      X = 1234567.
      DO 10 I = 1,1000
  10  X = X + .01
      WRITE(3,101) X
 101  FORMAT(' X=',F9.0)
      CALL EXIT
      END
```

The straightforward mathematical result should be 1234577., since we have added 0.01 one thousand times thus increasing the value of X by 10.0. However, if this program was run on an IBM 360 which with single precision real arithmetic has approximately 7 decimal digits of accuracy, the result would be 1234567. The value of X has not been altered because 0.01 was too small compared to 1234567. If we rewrote the program in DOUBLE PRECISION the result would be accurate.

```
      DOUBLE PRECISION X
      X = 1234567.D00
      DO 10 I = 1,1000
  10  X = X + 0.01D00
      WRITE(3,101) X
 101  FORMAT (' X=',F9.0)
      CALL EXIT
      END
```

DOUBLE PRECISION arithmetic can often be used to improve the accuracy of numerical results but it is no guarantee of correctness. Certainly the 56-bit mantissa in an IBM 360/370 DOUBLE PRECISION word is better than a 24-bit mantissa in a REAL word, but regardless of the finite word length used there is always some situation in which it will not be sufficiently long to guarantee accuracy.

The following hardware-dependent program can be used to determine the number of bits in the mantissa of the machine you are using. Understanding its operations will also give more of an insight into the nature of REAL arithmetic and the problems that are encountered.

```
      X = 1.0/2.0
      DO 10 I = 1,500
      Y = X + 1.0/2.0 ** (I + 1)
      IF (X .EQ. Y) GO TO 20
  10  X = Y
  20  WRITE(3,101) I
 101  FORMAT (' THIS COMPUTER HAS A MANTISSA ',I3,' BITS LONG.')
      CALL EXIT
      END
```

Smaller and smaller values are added to location X until the addition of another value does not change X. At that point the range of the machine's accuracy has been exceeded and we know how long the mantissa is. As we add larger negative powers of two we change a single bit each time until we exceed the accuracy and subsequent additions would not affect the value of X.

Difference of Similar Numbers and Division by Small Values

Problems may occur in taking the difference of two numbers which are approximately equal. For example, on an IBM 360

```
      A = 345678.9
      B = 345678.8
      C = A - B
      WRITE(3,101) C
101 FORMAT (' C=',F12.7)
```

produces

```
   C=  0.1250000
```

More disturbing is the result of dividing a large value by the difference of two numbers which are similar in value:

```
      A = 345678.9
      B = 345678.8
      D = 10000.0/(A - B)
      WRITE(3,101) D
101 FORMAT(' D=',F12.4)
```

We would expect the result to be 100000.00 but unfortunately the roundoff error on the division causes the value of D to be

```
   D=  80000.00
```

Overflow, Underflow, and Division by Zero

If the result of a mathematical operation has an exponent which exceeds the range of permitted exponents, it is not possible to store the value. If the exponent is too large we have an overflow; if the exponent is too small (too large a negative exponent) we have an underflow. The following program could not be run properly on an IBM 360/370 which accepts numbers ranging in magnitude from 16^{-65} (approximately 10^{-78}) to 16^{63} (approximately 10^{75}):

```
A = 8.0E50
B = 6.0E40
C = A * B
```

Overflow would occur since the expected result, 48.E90, is beyond the range of acceptable exponents, and an error message would be printed by the operating system.

Using double precision would not help here because double precision exponents have the same range as single precision exponents. The only solution is to reduce the size of the exponents (scale the values) and to keep track of them in the program.

```
    AA = A/1.0E50
    BB = B/1.0E45
    CC = AA * BB
    IEXP = 95
    WRITE(6,101)CC,IEXP
101 FORMAT (' C=',F6.0,'E',I3)
```

This technique presupposes that the values of the exponents are known or can be determined by the program. An extra burden is placed on the programmer, but the extra work must be done to arrive at the correct result.

In some cases, reordering the operations can prevent overflow or underflow. Consider the following program fragment:

```
   A = 7.0E-65
   B = 6.0E-24
   C = 2.0E+56
C        THE TRUE VALUE OF D IS 42.E-89
   D = A * B
C        THE TRUE VALUE OF E IS 84.E-33
   E = D * C
```

Underflow would occur when A was multiplied by B and although the result is not beyond the capacity of the hardware this sequence of computations would not be permitted. However, by rearranging the operations, the result 84.E−33 could be arrived at as follows:

```
C           THE TRUE VALUE OF DD IS 14.E09
       DD = A * C
C           THE TRUE VALUE OF EE IS 84.E−33
       EE = DD * B
```

Division by extremely small quantities may result in overflow; or roundoff errors. Division by *zero* produces an error because the operation is not defined. To prevent these errors the division should be tested before it is attempted:

```
   IF (ABS(DIVSOR) .LT. 1.0E−50) GO TO 30
   QUOTNT = DIVDND/DIVSOR
          .
          .
          .
30 WRITE(3,101) DIVDND,DIVSOR
101 FORMAT (' **** DIVISION ATTEMPTED WITH DIVIDEND =',
   1           E16.8,' AND DIVISOR=',E16.8)
```

It is difficult to suggest what you should do at this point, but at least there is a record of what transpired when this situation arose. One alternative is simply to terminate the run and try to find out why the condition occurred.

Output Roundoff

Even if there is no significant roundoff error in the computation of a mathematical result, the printed result may be inaccurate or deceiving. Consider the following program fragment:

```
          •
          •
          •
      WRITE(3,101)A,B,C
101   FORMAT(' A=',F4.1,' B=',F4.1,' C=',F4.1)
          •
          •
          •
      D = A/(B - C)
          •
          •
          •
      WRITE(3,102) D
102   FORMAT(' D=',F4.1)
```

which produces this output

```
A= 8.2 B= 4.6 C= 4.5
D=41.8
```

Looking at the first line of output and performing the calculation of D by hand, we might get

$$D = \frac{8.2}{4.6 - 4.5} = 82.$$

and would be surprised to find that the machine has printed 41.8.

The error was not produced by roundoff error in the calculation of the results, but by the roundoff of the values when they were printed. The output values of A, B, and C have been symmetrically rounded, and the hand calculations were not sufficiently accurate. If the F4.1 format fields were replaced by F7.4 fields, the output might be

```
A= 8.2000 B= 4.6475 C= 4.4513
D=41.7941
```

Now if the calculations were carried out the result would be justified:

$$D = \frac{8.2000}{4.6475 - 4.4513} = 41.7941$$

The user bears the responsibility for knowing the number of significant digits in his inputs and how many can be expected in the result. Printing excess digits in a result is equally sinful. If the input data has 3 significant digits, using a E14.7 field to print the results of a computation can only confuse those who interpret the output.

SUCCESSIVE ADDITIONS

A common computational task is to sum a series of values. The accumulated roundoff error may be large unless special precautions are taken. The difficulty arises when small terms are added onto an increasingly large partial sum. To get an idea of how serious the problem can be, let us add up 0.01 ten thousand times.

```
      SUM = 0.0
      DO 10 I = 1,10000
 10 SUM = SUM + 0.01
```

Printing out the value of SUM, we get 99.9527, not 100.0000. However, we can increase the accuracy by creating sub-sums and then adding these together. In the following rewritten program we sum up 100 values at a time and then combine them:

```
      SUM = 0.0
      DO 30 J = 1,100
      SUBSUM = 0.0
      DO 20 I = 1,100
 20 SUBSUM = SUBSUM + 0.01
 30 SUM = SUM + SUBSUM
```

Now if we print SUM we find that it is 99.99870, not perfect but somewhat improved. Taking smaller clusters of sums will improve the result but since 0.01 cannot be represented perfectly we cannot expect a perfect result. *Roundoff error can be reduced if the values added are of similar magnitudes.*

The same rule can be applied to summing infinite series such as

$$1 + \frac{1}{3} + \frac{1}{9} + \frac{1}{27} + \frac{1}{81} + \frac{1}{243} + \cdots$$

Mathematically, the result is the same whether we add up the large terms first or the small terms first, but when working with a finite word length machine there is a difference.

Adding forward 10 terms we get 1.499987 but summing backwards (i.e., taking the smaller terms first) we get 1.499991. The sum of the above infinite series should be precisely 3/2.

As a final example consider the infinite series

$$\frac{1}{1} + \frac{1}{2} + \frac{1}{3} + \frac{1}{4} + \frac{1}{5} + \cdots$$

which diverges to infinity. The following table shows the difference in the results when summing forward and when summing backward. As more and more terms are included the difference between the two methods becomes greater but in either case we are far from finding an infinite result and never could. Eventually we would exceed the capacity of the machine and no matter how many terms we added going forward the value of the sum would be unchanged. We would do better going backward, but even so we would eventually get an underflow in calculating one of the terms.

Number of terms	Summing forward	Summing backward
10	0.29289656E 01	0.29289675E 01
100	0.51873398E 01	0.51873646E 01
1000	0.74850149E 01	0.74852972E 01
10000	0.97828856E 01	0.97857227E 01
100000	0.12042140E 01	0.12070920E 01
1000000	0.13971106E 02	0.14207115E 02

NUMERICAL ANALYSIS

Researchers in the field of numerical analysis, which has been defined as the art of finding numerical solutions to problems when analytic techniques fail, spend a great deal of time worrying about the effect of roundoff errors. The goal of numerical analysis is to find algorithms which solve a problem in the shortest time with the greatest accuracy.

This text is not a guide to the theoretical analysis of error propagation in numerical analysis. There are a large number of books which cover the field adequately. For beginners we suggest

S. D. Conte, *Elementary Numerical Analysis*, McGraw-Hill, New York, 1965.

Peter Stark, *Introduction to Numerical Methods*, Macmillan, London, 1970.

Both have a simple, easy-to-read format and give FORTRAN programs for many of the algorithms presented. On a more advanced level we refer you to

Anthony Ralston, *A First Course in Numerical Analysis*, McGraw-Hill, New York, 1965.

Eugene Isaacson and Herbert Bishop Keller, *Analysis of Numerical Methods*, John Wiley, New York, 1966.

These texts provide a comprehensive guide to sophisticated techniques, careful analyses of error propagation, and thorough discussions of convergence criterion.

Checklist

INTEGER arithmetic
- Have you used mode conversion and truncation to ensure symmetric rounding when performing INTEGER division?
- Do you validate your data to avoid arithmetic overflow?

REAL arithmetic
- Do you allow for inaccuracy in the internal representation of decimal numbers?
- Do you avoid comparing REAL numbers for equality?
- Do you avoid performing arithmetic on numbers whose magnitudes differ greatly?
- Do you avoid performing subtractions on numbers which are approximately equal?
- Have you allowed for the possibility of overflow, underflow, and division by zero?

Roundoff errors
- Have you allowed sufficient width in output fields to print all significant fractional digits.
- Have you made your output fields too large and allowed extraneous digits to be printed?
- Have you clustered your summands in a summation to minimize roundoff?
- Do you perform summations on infinite series backwards to minimize roundoff error?

CHAPTER **5**

DOCUMENTATION

INTRODUCTION

Walk into any supermarket and you will see an amazing variety of packages, each protecting, delivering, informing, and displaying the contents within. Packaging is important and yet, if you are like most programmers, you don't think of the packaging of your program — the documentation. Like the instructions accompanying an appliance or piece of machinery, documentation teaches the recipient how to use and repair the product.

The amount of documentation which should be included with a program depends on the program's expected life, complexity, and distribution. Each case is unique but here are some guidelines:

Always provide more documentation than you think you need.

Chances are that the program will have a longer life and a wider distribution than your original expectations. Consider the extreme case: a "one shot" program for your own use. At the very least, document such a program with comments and meaningful variable names. The program may require extensive debugging, may later be used as the basis for a new program, or may be requested by someone else.

Document as much of the program within the code as possible.

This will concentrate the documentation where it will do the most good. If the documentation remains with the program, comments and code may be modified at the same time.

Document unto others as you would be documented to.

Programming can be fun, so can cryptography; however, they should not be combined. Obviously, *you* understand the purpose behind every statement in your program. If you make the recipient equally aware of the logic you employed he too will understand. It is as simple as that.

Be neat.

A neatly written program is easier to read and understand than a sloppy one.

Our general rules for documenting, then, are

- provide adequate documentation
- document within the program where possible
- be considerate
- be neat

Now, let us examine some specific documentation techniques applicable to FORTRAN programs.

IDENTIFYING FORTRAN STATEMENTS

The identification field of the FORTRAN card (columns 73-80) may be used for three purposes:

1. To identify the program
2. To sequence the cards
3. To flag modifications or special insertions

Columns 73-76 are available for use in identifying a particular sub-routine or program. We suggest that sequence numbering be restricted to columns 77-80. This procedure allows for decks of up to 1000 cards with sequence numbers incremented by 10. Numbering by tens permits insertions to be made without resequencing the entire deck. For example, a FUNCTION subprogram to find the average of an array of values could be identified as follows:

```
      FUNCTION AVERAG(X,N)              AVER0010
      DIMENSION X(1)                    AVER0020
      SUM = 0.0                         AVER0030
      DO 10 I = 1,N                     AVER0040
      SUM = SUM + X(I)                  AVER0050
   10 CONTINUE                          AVER0060
      AVERAG = SUM/N                    AVER0070
      RETURN                            AVER0080
      END                               AVER0090
```

If it later becomes necessary to make a modification such as a test for negative numbers, it could be inserted with, for example, sequence number 0045:

```
   IF ( X(I) .LT. 0.0) GO TO 10     AVER0045
```

Modifications or special versions of a program can be flagged in the identification field with the code word MOD and the date.

```
      IF (NOFICA)40,50,50               MOD06/21
   40 TAXRTE = 16.4                     MOD06/21
   50 CONTINUE                          MOD06/21
```

Temporary statements inserted for debugging purposes should be indicated by the use of the word DEBUG possibly followed by a sequence number.

```
      WRITE(6,801)MANNO,IRATE,ISALRY  DEBUG010
  801 FORMAT (' INPUT VALUE',3I10)     DEBUG020
```

These statements produce printout for debugging purposes only and may be removed once a reliable production version is complete.

Suspicious programmers (defined as those who suspect that a program is never fully debugged) leave the DEBUG cards in the deck, but put a "C" in column one, converting them into comment cards.

INSERTING COMMENTS

The comment card is one of the most powerful documentation tools available. *Meaningful* comments, strategically placed, can remove all doubt about the programmer's intentions when writing a particular statement. Carefully written comments enhance a program's usefulness and its ability to be modified. Consider the following comment in the context of the statement which it explains:

```
C
C           INCREMENT  I  BY  J
C
        I  =  I  +  J
```

Such a comment might just as well not be written. How much more meaningful is

```
C
C       SET  I  TO  THE  MAXIMUM  ALLJWABLE  SUBSCRIPT
C
     I  =  I  +  J
```

Notice that the second comment is valid only in the context of a specific program, whereas the first comment is valid in any context. The first comment tells the reader nothing that is not obvious from the syntax of the following statement; the second comment tells the reader the meaning of the statement which follows.

Comments are free format with the exception of the identifying "C" which always appears in column one. The comment should not extend beyond column 72 to avoid interfering with card sequencing.

Some programmers always begin in columns 3, 4, or 5 so that the comments stand out. Others prefer to begin in columns 10, 11, or 12 so that the comments don't interfere with a quick scan of the statement labels or the statements. Some begin comments in column 7 with their FORTRAN statements. Still other programmers are irregular and begin comments in different columns each time — we call this technique sloppy. Select a rule that suits you and stick to it.

```
C               SOLVE THE RESULTING LINEAR EQUATION
C
        ROOT = -B/A
        Y = FUNCT(ROOT)
        IF (Y .LT. 0.0) GO TO 40
        Y2 = Y*Y
C
C               READ THE NEXT EQUATION
C
        READ(5,400) A,B
```

Comments can also be preceded by two asterisks or two periods to help them stand out. For example,

```
        X = Y + 7.0
        Z = F(X) + G(Y)
C
C  ...      NOW USE THE MACHINE LOAD VALUE TO COMPUTE THE
C  ...      WORK SCHEDULE FOR THE CURRENT DAY.
C
        SHIFT = Z/8.0
        WORKV = ISTAFF * SHIFT
              .
              .
              .
```

It is good practice to surround comment cards by blank comment cards to increase readability.

Another useful technique is to enclose headings and titles in a frame of asterisks:

```
C
C        *****************************
C        *                           *
C        *   PROGRAM INITIALIZATION   *
C        *                           *
C        *****************************
C
```

This makes it very easy for the reader to locate relevant segments of code in a large program.

Prologue

Just as the prologue of a book introduces the reader to the content which follows, each program and subroutine should contain a prologue to introduce the reader to the routine which follows. COBOL, the business-oriented programming language, has a mandatory prologue called the *identification division*. The concept may be extended to FORTRAN by use of comments cards. The most important sections of the prologue are

program id	what program is this
author	who wrote it
date or revision	when was it written
description	what does it do and how does it do it
subroutines required	what other subroutines are needed

Consider the following example:

```
C
C     PROGRAM - SIMEQ
C
C     .PROGRAMMER - N.E. NAIM
C     DATE - JULY 1685
C
C     DESCRIPTION - THIS PROGRAM SOLVES A MATRIX OF SIMULTANEOUS
C     LINEAR EQUATIONS UP TO 20 BY 20.  THE METHOD USED IS GAUSS
C     ELIMINATION WITH MAXIMIZATION OF THE PIVOTAL COEFFICIENT.
C
C     SUBROUTINES - THIS PROGRAM USES SUBROUTINE RCIN TO FIND THE
C     MAXIMUM COEFFICIENT AND INTERCHANGE THE ROWS AND COLUMNS.
C
```

This prologue provides a very good idea of what the program does, what routines are called, who wrote the program, and what technique is used — a tremendous amount of information in fewer than 20 lines.

If the prologue is to a subroutine, two entries should be added — the calling sequence description and the possible error returns. For example, if the preceding prologue were to a subroutine we might add

```
C
C     CALLING SEQUENCE -  FLAG = SIMEQ(E,N,B)
C     WHERE E IS AN N BY N MATRIX CONTAINING THE COEFFICIENTS
C             OF THE EQUATIONS IN REAL MODE
C
C           N IS THE INTEGER NUMBER OF EQUATIONS TO BE SOLVED
C
C           B IS A REAL N ELEMENT VECTOR WHICH WILL CONTAIN THE
C             SOLUTIONS
C
C     NOTE - THE ARRAY E IS DESTROYED DURING THE SOLUTION
C
C     RETURN CODES - FLAG = 0.0 IF A SOLUTION WAS FOUND
C                    FLAG = 1.0 IF N WAS NOT BETWEEN 1 AND 20
C                    FLAG = -1.0 IF NO SOLUTION WAS FOUND
C
```

There are many other possible inclusions for a program's prologue. The specifics must, as always, be left to the programmer's craftsmanship and creativity. The authors believe that the prologues presented here represent a reasonable minimum requirement for all programs; the only way to move is up.

Listing Variable Names

Programmers may use a number of mnemonic variable names which are difficult to keep track of or may not be obvious to others. To make clear exactly what each variable stands for and its function, the programmer should list each variable used with the problem-related description. Consider this brief example:

```
C
C     AVG      AVERAGE OF THE VALUES
C     N        NUMBER OF VALUES IN ARRAY XVAL
C     STDDEV   STANDARD DEVIATION OF THE VALUES
C     XVAL     ARRAY OF VALUES FROM EXPERIMENT
C
```

Insertion Before Loops

It is safe to say that almost every DO loop should be preceded by comments. The reason is that a DO loop and its terminating statement form a sort of parentheses around some computational function; it is this function which should be documented. For example,

```
C
C          SET THE TABLES TO 0.0 BEFORE PROCESSING
C
       DO 10 I = 1,N
       A(I) = 0.0
       B(I) = 0.0
       C(I) = 0.0
    10 CONTINUE
```

To accentuate the parenthetical effect of a DO statement, it is usually best to use the CONTINUE statement to close the loop.

CHOOSING VARIABLE NAMES

A FORTRAN variable has two attributes of interest: *mode* and *value*. By *mode* we mean the type of values which the variable may assume. For example, REAL variables may assume any value representable as a floating point number, INTEGER variables may only assume integral values, and LOGICAL variables have a range of true and false. The *value* of a variable is its contents at a given instant during the execution of the program.

Variable names should be chosen with care; the name should indicate the variable's mode and value. A poor choice of variable name will significantly decrease the program's intelligibility. To illustrate how much information can be conveyed by proper choice of variable name, consider the following examples:

Replace This	*With this*
A = B * C	RATE = DIST * TIME
A = B * C	SALARY = WAGE * HOURS
Q = S(D)	Y = F(X)
Q = S(D)	SCORE = X(I)
B = ALPHA/BETA	AVERAG = SUM/N

In the above examples, the second column conveys much more information than the first although the corresponding statements in each column are (or could be) equivalent. In general,

> *express the mode of a variable by its first letter and express the value of a variable by the rest of the name.*

Mode

In the statement

$$A = B ** (C/D(E))$$

the computations performed depend upon the modes of the variables. FORTRAN has a default convention that variables beginning with the letters I, J, K, L, M, and N are of INTEGER mode and all others are of REAL mode unless declared otherwise.

This convention is based upon mathematical tradition in which the letters I-N are used as subscripts. The I-N convention has become well established and has been used by other programming languages. When a FORTRAN programmer reads a statement such as

$$A = I$$

he automatically assumes that the variable A is real and the variable I is integer; to disregard this convention is to confuse.

The mode conventions may well be extended to other types of variables. COMPLEX variables may be preceded by a "C," LOGICAL variables by an "L" (or a "B" for *Boolean*), and DOUBLE PRECISION variables by a "D." This practice follows the same rules as the FORTRAN library functions (for example, SQRT becomes DSQRT in double precision).

Following the conventions outlined above will improve the comprehensibility of the program.

PRODUCING A NEAT PROGRAM

A neat program, that is a program with an uncluttered listing, is much easier to read than a sloppy program. Neatness is not difficult to achieve if you follow these rules:

- Begin every statement in column 7 unless you are within a DO loop. With a DO loop indent two columns for every level of DO. For example,

```
      DO 30 I = 1,N
        DO 20 J = 1,N
        SUM = 0.0
          DO 10 K = 1,N
          SUM = SUM + A(I,K)*B(K,J)
10        CONTINUE
        IC(I,J) = SUM + 0.5
20      CONTINUE
      WRITE(6,101) I,(IC(M), M = 1,N)
30 CONTINUE
```

Note that the statement labels are right-justified for readability.
- FORMAT statements may either be written after the READ or WRITE which references them or collected together at the end of the program. In general, the first alternative is preferable since it eliminates a search.
- Arithmetic and logical operators should be surrounded by blanks (with the possible exception of /). This will make statements easier to read. Avoid constructions like

```
      IF(A+3..GT..5) GO TO 50
```

in deference to

```
      IF ( A + 3.0  .GT. 0.5) GO TO 50
```

- Arrange statement labels in ascending order so that a reader of your program will not need to search for a statement. Reserve specific ranges of numbers for executable statement labels and FORMAT statement labels; for example, use the labels 1 through 999 for executable statements and 1000 or above for FORMATs. Labels beginning with the digits "99" could indicate termination points:

```
  10  READ(5,1000) N
1000  FORMAT(I3)
      IF (N .EQ. 0) GO TO 99
      DO 20 I = 1,N
      J = I*I
      WRITE(6,1010) I,J
1010  FORMAT(4H I= , I3, 4H J= , I3)
  20  CONTINUE
      GO TO 10
  99  WRITE(6,1020)
1020  FORMAT(28H **INVALID N. RUN TERMINATED)
      CALL EXIT
      END
```

- Never break up a variable name or a constant between two cards. Avoid statements like

```
      RATE = DIST * TI
    1ME
```

- When you continue a statement onto a new card, indent the continuation so that similar parts of the statement line up.

For example,

```
      A = A1 * X +
    1     B1 * Y +
    2     C1 * Z
            .
            .
            .
 2000 FORMAT (1H0,I7,F13.4,A1,10X,
    1          I7,F14.7,20X,I3)
```

Note that in the first example above, the continuation card is implied by the terminating "+"; this provides some protection since the loss of the card

```
    2     C1 * Z
```

from the deck would result in a syntax error.

- If you really want to produce a neat program, alphabetize the variable names in your declaration statements and line them up in columns:

```
COMMON  AVALUE,B       ,CDATE ,DEPT  ,
1            FICA   ,GTDATE,HOURS  ,WAGES ,
2            YTDATE
```

Many programmers begin their programs neatly but fail to continue the habit during the process of modification and debugging. A number of FORTRAN "clean-up" programs are available which reformat a source program in accordance with the rules specified in this section. The use of these programs, when available, is recommended.

ORGANIZING PROGRAM OUTPUT

Documentation is not confined to program source code; there must be adequate documentation of the output in order for it to be intelligible. Two questions should be answered for every number appearing in the program's printed output: what is the name of the number and what is the number's value. Although these questions may seem simple, their answers are important if the output is to be understandable. The name of a number may be indicated by preceding the printed number with an alphabetic label. This is so obvious that it is almost embarrassing to mention it, and yet we have seen many programs with numbers floating aimlessly about on the output pages, their identity a long forgotten secret. It is safe to say that a number should never appear without a label on output.

The second consideration, the value of a number, is also important. Computers are able to perform arithmetic with accuracy and a number produced by a computer has credibility. This credibility is often abused by programmers who imbue their data with false significance by printing too many digits on their output. Since computers work in fixed units of one (or more) words, a computer will print digits when requested even if these have no meaning. There are two cases where this may arise. The first occurs when the data, itself, lacks accuracy. Suppose, for example, a student has two test grades. If the following program fragment were executed:

```
      READ (5,1000) SCORE1,SCORE2
 1000 FORMAT (2F2.0)
      AVERGE = (SCORE1 + SCORE2)/2.
      WRITE (6,2000) AVERGE
 2000 FORMAT (17H THE AVERAGE IS   ,F10.6)
```

the result

```
      THE AVERAGE IS    83.483275
```

might be obtained. The data does not have eight significant digits and yet the computer will compute and print the results as though the last digits were meaningful. *Numbers which are the result of computations cannot have more significant digits than the data from which they are derived.* Incorrect results may also be inadvertently printed when the accumulated error of the computation causes a loss of significance. This can be most serious since absolute garbage may appear quite meaningful to the unwary.

Frequently a program encounters an error or questionable condition. It is good practice in these cases to print an error message in order to warn the reader of the situation. Whether to terminate the run must, of course, be determined for each case. Error messages should provide the reader with as much information as possible. It is a good idea to associate a unit identifier with every error message. We suggest the following:

$$* * * * *PPPNNN - \text{text}$$

where

> The asterisks serve to set off the error message from other output.
> PPP is a program identification which indicates the program or subroutine which produced the error message.
> NNN is a unique three-digit identification.

The three-digit qualifier may be used to differentiate between various messages which have the same text. For example, the messages

```
* * * * *XYZ001 - ATTEMPT TO DIVIDE BY ZERO.

* * * * *XYZ002 - ATTEMPT TO DIVIDE BY ZERO.
```

indicate two different errors. The specific error may be determined by inspection of the source listing. The use of non-unique text is not recommended if it is possible to more precisely specify the error but this is often difficult.

If the error is preceded by a message identification as described above, it may be worthwhile to construct a listing of error messages and their meanings for the users of the program. An excellent example of this type of book is the IBM System 360 Messages and Codes Manual. Entries in an error listing should be keyed on the message number and may follow a format similar to the one described below:

XYZ001 *Message*:   XYZ001 — ATTEMPT TO DIVIDE BY ZERO.
      Meaning: The value of the function has become zero. This probably indicates invalid input data.
      Action: The division is bypassed and the results stored as 99999E+50.

EXTERNAL DOCUMENTATION

In addition to the documentation in the program, external documentation is good practice. Such documentation is of particular importance for large, complex programs which are part of a group of programs in a sophisticated system such as a banking or inventory management system. The relationship of one program to the entire system should be described including the formats of inputs and outputs. For large programs it is not unusual for the programmer to create a complete book of external documentation. Information in such a book should fall into two categories: (1) details describing how to use the program; (2) specifics of the internal operation of the program.

There is no limit to the extent of external documentation. The following checklist is a minimum:

- programmer identification
- minimum machine and operating system configuration required to run this job
- special forms used for input or output
- mountables required — tapes, disks, data cells, etc.

- operator's run book — a guide to the operator describing how to run this program including error conditions and required actions.
- reference to related programs which provide input to this program or use the output
- reference to special reports or journal articles describing sophisticated mathematical or programming techniques used

Checklist

Program sequencing
- Have you sequenced your FORTRAN statements, incrementing the number in each card by 10?

Comments
- Have you placed meaningful comments throughout the program?
- Does your program have a prologue composed of comments cards?
- Have you surrounded your comments by blank cards and do all comments begin in column 10?

Variable Names
- Do your variable names begin with letters which indicate their mode?
- Are all your variable names meaningful?

Neatness
- Is your program neat and easy to read?
- Have you used blanks around arithmetic and logical operators?
- Are your statement labels in ascending order?

Output
- Is your output neat and easy to read?
- Does every number have a label or heading?
- Have you included meaningful error messages in your program?

External documentation
- Do you have any?
- Why not?

CHAPTER 6

PROGRAM DESIGN

INTRODUCTION

The design and organization of a program is a very personal experience. Every programmer has his own way of going about the development process. Programming is still an art, but even artists have rules of composition and style. We have isolated four design goals which programmers should consider in creating a program.

1. *Modularity*, the logical segmentation of a program into subroutines, is desirable since it aids the organizational clarity, the "debug-ability," and the "modify-ability" of a program.
2. *Independence*, the freedom from unique machine, compiler, or operating system features, affects the ease with which a program may be run in another environment.
3. *Generality*, the flexibility of the coding to accept slightly varying inputs, determines how useful a program will be.
4. *Integrity*, a measure of how thoroughly a programmer has considered the implications of unexpected input data, determines how reliable a program will be.

Unfortunately, these four design goals are not independent. An attempt to enhance the independence of a program may reduce the generality. Improving the integrity of a program may add to the complexity and interfere with modularity. Once again, the programmer must consider his working environment and determine which design goals are dominant.

MODULARITY

When should you write a segment of code as a subroutine? There are two cases:

1. When the segment performs a well-defined sequence of operations which is repeated several times in the program.
2. When the segment performs a well-defined function, but the code is potentially less or more stable than other parts of the program.

In designing a program you always create a flowchart. Perhaps you only do this mentally, but before you write a line of code you must consider the sequencing of operations. As you design a program, the blocks of the macro flowchart (or system flowchart) are expanded as the details become more well defined. Finally, the blocks of the micro flowchart are clarified and converted into program code. The blocks of the macro flowchart should be considered subroutines. Subroutines represent a higher level logical organization of your program.

To give meaning to these abstract considerations, consider this example. A program is to be written to compare two files of data and determine if specific fields of corresponding records of each file are equal. If the fields do not match, then both records are to be printed. The logic of this program is extremely simple, yet this type of program can be expanded to include a variety of special cases and exceptions. It is the type of utility program which often has a long lifetime and a wide distribution and is susceptible to a wide range of modifications. At the outset the following design goals should be set:

1. The program should be as general as possible, using control or parameter cards to determine the number and position of the fields to be compared.
2. The program should be as modular as possible to simplify modification and expansion.

Accordingly, the following macroflowchart is reasonable:

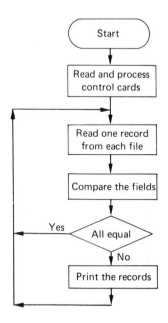

Each of the boxes in the macroflowchart can be written as a subroutine. Communication among the various routines should be accomplished via a labeled COMMON. The main program of the compare program is then almost trivial:

```
      COMMON /COMP/...,UNEQ,...
      LOGICAL UNEQ
C
C        READ CONTROL CARDS
C
      CALL CNTRLS
C
C        READ A RECORD FROM EACH FILE
C
   10 CALL READ12
C
C     CHECK IF ALL FIELDS ARE EQUAL. IF NOT, PRINT RECORDS.
C
      CALL COMPAR
      IF (UNEQ) CALL PRINT
      GO TO 10
      END
```

This program is a good example of modularity. Note the following points:

- The control card analysis and record printout are not critical to the logic of the program; however, both require considerable code. They are also quite likely to change in time. During the initial debugging, they can be written as minimal routines and later replaced by more sophisticated subprograms.
- Although many fields might have to be compared and even one failure is sufficient to cause a record to be rejected, only one *global* switch, UNEQ, is used to transmit the information.
- The main program conveys the logic of the overall program. A person who wished to modify a segment of the program need not be concerned with more than one routine since all changes are isolated.
- The work in developing the program could be split among several programmers each working separately. They would have to agree only on the order and the contents of variables in the COMMON field.
- If overlaying were necessary, it would be easy to perform.

A more sophisticated example of the modularization of a large program is the macro flowchart for a compiler.

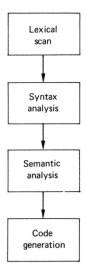

Lexical scan is the check for illegal characters and the conversion of groups of characters into *tokens*. A token is a single grammatical or syntactic entity such as a keyword, a variable, or a constant. Syntactic analysis is the checking of the clusters of tokens to determine whether they represent a valid assignment statement, subroutine call, or I/O statement. Semantic analysis is an intermediate stage which converts a recognized source language statement into an internal form for use during code generation. Only during the last step is any object language statement produced. Thus if it were desired to convert a compiler to produce code for another computer, only the code generation stage would have to be changed.

The addition of a code optimization section would not require a complete rewriting of the program. The output from the semantic analysis stage could be examined by a code optimizing program and the results could be fed to the code generator.

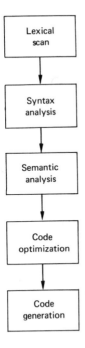

Large sophisticated programs are not built in a day — they evolve through many versions and modifications. A well-designed modular program can easily grow and be improved.

INDEPENDENCE

The independence of a program is a measure of how easily it may be run under a different compiler, operating system, or computer. The more independent a program is, the easier it is to transfer it to a new environment. Certainly, a program or subroutine destined for wide distribution should have a high degree of independence.

Creating a program which is independent requires a detailed knowledge of the compilers, operating systems, and hardware in use and increases the programmer's burden. More disturbingly, the advantages of a particular environment cannot be utilized since these special facilities may not be available under other conditions.

The rules we present are not firm rules which must never be violated: they are guidelines. Again, the programmer must weigh the tradeoffs in each case and decide on the benefits of each route. The general considerations are

- Do I expect this program to be used in other environments? If so, how varied will these environments be?
- Is the additional coding and debugging effort worth the independence gained?
- How much additional run time and storage will be used if I create an independent program?
- How will the clarity of the program be impaired?

The techniques of creating an independent program are difficult to isolate. A good starting point is to adhere to the ANSI definition of Basic FORTRAN IV (Report X3.10-1966) which most manufacturers specify will be accepted by their production compilers. The subset is restrictive, but it should be possible to code all FORTRAN IV programs within the bounds of this language definition.

Beyond this general rule, the following restrictions should be adhered to even if your environment permits them to be violated:

- The maximum length of variables should be five alphanumeric characters. Do not use "$" as an alphabetic character.
- Do not use DATA or labeled COMMON.

- Use only the arithmetic IF statement; avoid the logical IF statement.
- Do not use the PRINT or PUNCH statements; stick to the READ (unit, format) and WRITE (unit, format) statements.
- Use only INTEGER, REAL, and DOUBLE PRECISION type declarations. Avoid COMPLEX, LOGICAL, INTEGER*n, REAL*n, CHARACTER, or IMPLICIT declarations.
- Avoid multiple entry SUBROUTINEs.
- Specify variables for I/O units so that they may be easily changed. For example,

```
IN = 1
JOUT = 3
READ(IN,1001) SALES
WRITE(JOUT,1002) PROFIT
```

- Keep one statement per card even if your present compiler permits more than one statement with a delimiter character.
- Avoid multiple substitutions such as

```
A = B = C = 0.0
```

- Avoid bit masks and bit operations such as

```
N = 07731 .AND. MASK
```

- Don't depend on special end-of-file tests such as

```
READ (5,1001,END = 999)
```

or

```
IF (EOF,5) 999,70
```

Instead, use a trailer card after the data to signal end-of-file conditions.
- Avoid octal or hexadecimal operations or printout.
- Use A1 formats for character input/output even if your computer hardware permits A4, A6, or A10 formats. Following this rule wastes a great deal of storage, so it should be carefully considered.

- Beware of large INTEGER values – they may overflow on another computer.
- Beware of extremely large or small REAL values – the exponents may overflow or underflow on another computer.
- Beware of accuracy. If a REAL computation is sensitive to the number of bits in the mantissa, the results may be different on another computer.
- Consider output line width. Most high speed printers have 132 characters per line but some are limited to 120 characters per line. Teletype or display terminals may have 80, 72, or fewer characters per line.
- On output, keep to the FORTRAN 48 character set even if your system permits other special characters.
- Use Hollerith fields in FORMAT statements. Many compilers permit literals to be enclosed within a pair of apostrophes or asterisks. These special features are extremely convenient since they eliminate the need to count the length but they are not universally accepted.
- Avoid arrays with more than two dimensions.
- Subscripts should be in one of the following seven formats:

$$v$$
$$c_1$$
$$c_1 * v$$
$$v + c_1$$
$$v - c_1$$
$$c_1 * v + c_2$$
$$c_1 * v - c_2$$

where v is a variable and c_1 and c_2 are INTEGER constants.
- Use only these carriage control characters:

$$1 \quad \text{new page}$$
$$0 \quad \text{skip two lines}$$
$$b \quad \text{skip one line}$$

- Limit the number of continuation cards to five per statement.
- In DO loops, the index variable, initial value, upper limit, and increment should all be unsubscripted INTEGER variables or posi-

tive INTEGER constants. Watch that the value of the index variable does not get large; some processors use less than a full word for the index variable.

- Avoid special error detection routines. Some compilers and operating systems provide extremely useful but nonstandard error detection routines.
- Do not use frec format output statements or NAMELIST — they are not standard.
- Do not permit special debug statements to remain permanently in a program.
- Avoid the assigned GO TO.

GENERALITY

Generality is a measure of how easily a program may be modified to perform a slightly different but closely related task. The major concern is the facility with which different input data sets may be accommodated. A plotting program would have a high degree of generality if it could

- produce any number of plots on the same set of axes
- handle any number of data points in any input format
- accept data over any range of values
- interpret INTEGER or REAL values
- accept positive or negative values
- scale axes (possibly even logarithmic scaling)
- optionally print titles or label axes
- optionally calculate and print interpolated points
- produce output for a line printer or cathode ray display or pen plotter

Including all of the above items would require an immense program most of whose facilties might never be used.

Once again, it is the programmer's professional responsibility to decide on the basis of his working environment, which options to include. Is the extra effort warranted or is it wasted time spent in pursuit of the elusive perfect program? Do the extra features result in an excessively large, complex, and slow "kludge"?

The techniques to make a program more general are dependent on the function of the particular program. If the program is designed to process a particular set of data items, it can usually be converted to accept a variable number of data items. A novice programmer might write the following code to process 37 data items:

```
      DIMENSION DATA(37)
      READ (1,1001)(DATA(I), I = 1,37)
 1001 FORMAT (10F8.2)
      DO 10 I = 1,37
           .
           .
           .
   10 CONTINUE
      WRITE (3,1002) (DATA(I) I = 1,37)
```

To alter this program to accept 38 items would require retyping and recompiling. With only a small additional effort a more general program could have been written:

```
      DIMENSION DATA(100)
      READ (1,1001) N,(DATA(I),I=1,N)
 1001 FORMAT (I3/(10F8.2))
      DO 10 I = 1,N
           .
           .
           .
   10 CONTINUE
      WRITE (3,1002) (DATA(I),I = 1,N)
```

This version accepts sets of data with 1 to 100 items and could accept larger sets by simply changing the DIMENSION statement. Instead of reading N from a single parameter or header card, there might have been a single trailer card which signified the end of data and the program could have done the counting to determine N. The trailer card technique eliminates the possibility of a mistake in counting the number of input cards and reduces the chance of errors.

The input format could be generalized so that data in formats other than 10F8.2 could be processed without altering the program. The use of object time FORMAT statements, when available, should be carefully considered since it places an extra burden not only on the programmer, but on the user of the program as well. The following version of our simple program uses an object time FORMAT in array NFORM:

```
      DIMENSION DATA(100),NFORM(10)
      READ (1,1000) N
 1000 FORMAT (I3)
      READ (1,1001) NFORM
 1001 FORMAT (10A4)
      READ (1,NFORM) (DATA(I),I = 1,N)
      DO 10 I = 1,N
         .
         .
         .
   10 CONTINUE
      WRITE (3,1003) (DATA(I),I = 1,N)
```

Object time formats can be used to give greater flexibility in controlling I/O operations. One of the limitations of FORTRAN is that the format specification can contain only constants; variables are not permitted. It is not possible to neatl_ output a rectangular array if the dimensions are determined at run time. We would like to write

```
      DIMENSION A(10,10)
         .
         .
         .
      NROWS=
      NCOLS=
         .
         .
         .
      WRITE(3,101) ((A(I,J),J=1,NCOLS), I = 1,NROWS)
  101 FORMAT (NCOLS(3X,F8.2)/)
```

but most dialects of FORTRAN prohibit formats with variables. This limitation can be overcome by some tricky handling of object time formats.

First read in the alphabetic values of the numbers up to the largest value expected, say 12. Then input the FORMAT desired leaving blank spaces to insert the correct number in character form. Once the proper FORMAT has been created, it can be used or altered as many times as needed. This example demonstrates the rectangular printing of the contents of the A array.

```
      DIMENSION A(10,10),NFMT(10),NUM(10)
      READ (1,101) NUM,NFMT
101   FORMAT (10A4/10A4)
           .
           .
           .
      NROWS=
      NCOLS=
           .
           .
           .
      NFMT(2) = NUM(NCOLS)
      WRITE(3,NFMT) ((A(I,J),J=1,NCOLS),I=1,NROWS
```

INPUT

```
    1    2    3    4    5    6    7    8    9   10
(          (3X,F8.2)/)
```

A basic technique for creating a general program is to read parameter or control cards which set flags or switches thus determining the operation of the program for a particular run. The idea is the same as the concept behind control cards for an operating system or a compiler. Different operations, inputs, or outputs can be determined by statements preceding a set of data items.

INTEGRITY

Integrity is a measure of the ability of a program to perform correctly on different sets of input. In a sense, integrity is a measure of how thoroughly a program has been tested and debugged. A program to sort numbers in ascending order which works fine for positive values but "bombs" for negative values or a program which loops infinitely if there are only 1 or 2 numbers to sort lacks integrity. Programs which exceed the declared size of an array for certain cases or do not test for division by zero also lack integrity.

If we could enumerate all the rules for building integrity into a program, we might be able to automate the debugging and program checkout stages. The best we can hope for is to suggest potentially dangerous situations and hope that programmers will carefully evaluate program areas.

Compilers can help the programmer by inserting code which checks if array subscripts are exceeded or if storage locations are referenced before they are set, but not all compilers provide such facilities. In any case, compilers cannot provide intelligible explanations of the cause of the failure. Furthermore, there may be errors which do not violate the programming semantics but which produce incorrect results. A keypunching mistake could turn a bank deposit of 30.00 dollars into a 3000.00 windfall. A program with a high degree of integrity should check input values to determine if they are within realistic bounds. For example, a student grading program should screen out all grades that are not in the range of 0 to 100. If an array manipulating subroutine is designed to handle up to 10 by 10 square arrays, then the input argument which specifies the size of the array should be tested to see that it is less than or equal to ten and greater than 1.

In debugging a program you should try to create combinations of input so that every branch of the program is tested. A large program such as a compiler or a complex simulation can never be fully tested and it is common to find bugs in such programs years after they have been released.

A special problem in FORTRAN is checking input data to determine if a field contains a blank or a one. Blanks are automatically converted into a zero internally by the I/O routines. To overcome this difficulty it would be convenient if we could read an input record twice, once as alphanumeric characters and again as numbers. For example, assume we had 80 one-digit INTEGER numbers ranging from 0 to 9 per card with a blank indicating the absence of data. By using the T format item, if available, we could re-scan the record and check each field for a blank.

```
   DIMENSION NUM(80),NALPHA(80)
   DATA NBLANK /1H /
   READ (5,101) NALPHA,NUM
101 FORMAT (80A1,T1,80I1)
```

Then if we want to average only those data values entered we could write

```
   NUM = 0
   N = 0
   DO 30 I = 1,80
   IF (NALPHA(I) .EQ. NBLANK) GO TO 30
   N = N + 1
   NSUM = NSUM + NUM(I)
30 CONTINUE
   IF (N .EQ. 0) GO TO 70
   AVERAG = FLOAT(NSUM)/FLOAT(N)
```

The following list contains some tests to ensure that programs won't go wrong.

- Check if the input parameters are in the expected range.
- Check subscripts to see if they are out of range of DIMENSION information.
- Test for inadvertent division by zero.
- Make sure that no variable is referenced before it is set.
- Test if input arguments to library functions are valid. Don't be surprised if you can't take the square root of a negative number using REAL arithmetic.
- If an array has a maximum size MAX, think about whether the program will perform properly with MAX, 1 or 0 locations filled.

Checklist

Modularity

- Are program segments whose functions are required in several places written as subroutines?

- Have you isolated, as subroutines, program segments which are likely to change?
- Have you used global switches to maintain status information among the various subroutines?

Independence
- Have you adhered to ANSI standard FORTRAN?
- Have you used A1 formats for alphanumeric information?
- Have you restricted the magnitude of the numbers you will be using so that overflow and underflow will not occur on a different computer?
- Is your output line width less than 121 characters?

Generality
- Have you used variables in preference to constants?
- Do you use switches to maintain status information?
- Is your program parameterized?

Integrity
- Do you check your input data for validity?
- Can your program handle unexpected data?
- Do you detect likely errors and signal them?
- Have you debugged your program using sufficient combinations of input data in order to test all paths?

SUGGESTIONS FOR FURTHER READING

(The abbreviation CACM refers to *Communications of the Association for Computing Machinery*, a monthly publication which reports on new developments in computer science.)

Cleary, J. G. "A FORTRAN Technique for Simplifying Input to Report Generators." *CACM* 9, No. 6 (June 1966), pp. 441–442.

A short note on a report generator program which calculates FORMAT statements for automatic report generation.

Fisher, D. L. "Data, Documentation and Decision Tables." *CACM* 9, No. 1 (January 1966), pp. 26–31.

A discussion of a method of defining and documenting files and decision criteria by a tabular structure.

Ford, *Basic FORTRAN IV Programming* Homewood, Illinois: Irwin, 1971.

A good introductory book on this commonly used subset of FORTRAN IV.

Forsythe, Alexandra I., Thomas A. Keenan, Elliot I. Organick, Warren Stenberg. *Computer Science: A First Course.* New York: John Wiley & Sons, Inc., 1969.
A well-organized text with lucid explanations of the basic principles of computing.

Larson, C. "The Efficient Use of FORTRAN." *Datamation* (August 1, 1971), pp. 24–31.
A discussion of techniques used to optimize FORTRAN programs. Most of the techniques mentioned are discussed in this book.

Linz, Peter. "Accurate Floating-Point Summation." *CACM* 13, No. 6 (June 1970), pp. 361–362.

Lowry, Edward, and C. W. Medlock. "Object Code Optimization." *CACM* 12, No. 1 (January 1969), pp. 13–22.
A rather technical discussion of the extensive optimization performed by the IBM System/360 "FORTRAN H" compiler.

McCracken, Daniel. *A Guide to FORTRAN IV Programming.* New York: John Wiley & Sons, Inc., 1965.
A good straightforward mathematically-oriented text.

Meissner, Loren P. *Rudiments of FORTRAN.* Reading, Mass.: Addison-Wesley Publishing Company, 1971.
A concise and quick introduction to the language.

Neely, Peter M. "Comparison of Several Algorithms for Computation of Means, Standard Deviations and Correlation Coefficients." *CACM* 9, No. 7 (July 1966).

Nolan, Richard L. *FORTRAN IV Computing and Applications.* Reading, Mass.: Addison-Wesley Publishing Company, 1971.
An excellent in-depth coverage of FORTRAN IV with a liberal arts or business student orientation.

Order, Alex. "The Emergence of a Profession." *CACM* 10, No. 9 (March 1967), pp. 145–148.
A nontechnical discussion of the emergence of the professional field of computer programming and some of its characteristics.

Organick, Elliot I. *A FORTRAN IV Primer*. Reading, Mass.: Addison-Wesley Publishing Company, 1966.
A good first book which includes the details of many dialects of FORTRAN IV.

Parker, Donn B. "Rules of Ethics in Information Processing." *CACM* 11, No. 3 (March 1968), pp. 198–201.
A discussion of the *Guidelines for Professional Conduct in Information Processing* adopted by the Association for Computing Machinery (ACM) in 1966.

Ralston, Anthony. *Introduction to Programming and Computer Science*. New York: McGraw-Hill Book Company, 1971.
A thorough in-depth introduction with good examples in FORTRAN, PL/I, ALGOL, and COBOL.

Silver, Gerald. *Simplified FORTRAN IV Programming*. New York: Harcourt Brace Jovanovich, Inc., 1971.
An easy introduction to FORTRAN programming for the non-mathematically-oriented student.

Stuart, Frederic. *FORTRAN Programming*. New York: John Wiley and Sons, Inc., 1970.
A wealth of reference material comparing the features of 152 different versions of the language.

USA Standard FORTRAN. ANSI Standard X 3.9–1966. New York: American National Standards Institute.

USA Standard Basic FORTRAN. ANSI Standard X 3.10–1966. New York: American National Standards Institute.
Definitions of the Standard FORTRAN language and a subset of standard FORTRAN called Standard Basic FORTRAN. Programs which adhere to the ANSI standards should compile on any FORTRAN compiler.

Veinott, Cyril G. "Programming Decision Tables in FORTRAN, COBOL or ALGOL." *CACM* 9, No. 1 (January 1966), pp. 32–35.
A presentation of the techniques of programming decision tables. This article should be of particular interest for those involved in business-oriented problems.

Walker, R. J. "Binary Summation." *CACM* 14, No. 6 (June 1971), p. 417.

A comment on a method of reducing the storage space required in utilizing the Linz method of summation cited above.

Westin, Alan F. "Legal Safeguards to Insure Privacy in a Computer Society." *CACM* 10, No. 9 (September 1967), pp. 533–537.

A nontechnical discussion of some of the legal aspects of computer "surveillance."

Wright, Donald. "A Comparison of the FORTRAN Language Implementation for Several Computers." *CACM* 9, No. 2 (February 1966), pp. 77–79.

A feature-by-feature comparison of the FORTRAN implementations for the following computers: IBM 7090/94, IBM 360, CDC 3000 series, and GE 400 series.

INDEX